Journey To Fellowship

by
Don Bounds

Bloomington, IN   Milton Keynes, UK
authorHOUSE®

AuthorHouse™
1663 Liberty Drive, Suite 200
Bloomington, IN 47403
www.authorhouse.com
Phone: 1-800-839-8640

AuthorHouse™ UK Ltd.
500 Avebury Boulevard
Central Milton Keynes, MK9 2BE
www.authorhouse.co.uk
Phone: 08001974150

First published by AuthorHouse 3/28/2007

ISBN: 978-1-4343-0405-6 (sc)

Library of Congress Control Number: 2007902255

Printed in the United States of America
Bloomington, Indiana

This book is printed on acid-free paper.

In Memoriam

Lora J. Bounds

Born in this world May 22, 1924 ---Crossed over December 24, 2006

This book is dedicated to the memory of a godly woman, my mother. The memory of her kind and gentle spirit shall live on. Her faith and spirit shall surely shine as a beacon to her family and those who viewed up close the life of my mother. And her works shall follow her. I understand what the Bible means when it states of a virtuous woman; "Her children shall rise up and call her blessed".As a child, I tended to view my mother as more stern and unyielding. But today I call her blessed! As I gained a maturity born of several years, my perspective gained depth. I was able to see the "real" things my mother had accomplished. Then, in my "life garden" where love of "mom" always existed, appreciation, and admiration grew in healthy abundance. My mother was a good woman.

She never considered her life extraordinary and would blush today if she thought I had said so. For you see, her extraordinary life is not characterized by accumulated wealth, an extended education, or corporate career. Why, she never even had a driver's license. What , you ask, could be extraordinary about her? In spite of what she did not have, my mother was a good mother.

My mother never held a full time job outside her home. But appeared content to do her full time work at home. Maybe strange, but I never heard her complain of boredom or an unfulfilled life. Her life was the Lord, the church, her husband, her four boys and other things. In that order! We were all the recipients of her love and industry. My mother was a good mother.

A single page is small allotment for memories of a lifetime. But in this remembrance, brevity is a necessity. Just like her 82 years, this page is swiftly filled. But not too filled to mention one last superlative in a life of self sacrifice and love. My mother never lost her hunger for truth. She was willing to pay the price of study, meditation and prayer. In so doing her soul was fed and her faith remained solidly anchored in that which she understood to be the word of God. My mother was a good woman.

My mother did not live to see this book completed. But I am thankful she was able to proofread (many times) all but the last few pages. Her words were encouraging and we rarely talked without her enquiring about "the book" and its completion. I marvel concerning her quest for, and interest in, the truth, even on difficult subjects. At an age when many lose their zest and interest in learning, she did not. I thank the Lord for sparing her mind even as the strength of body was waning. She was a mighty tower in this work and in the kingdom. May her reward be rich! My mother was a good mother.

To her (and my father), I'm indebted. A loving son.   Don B.

Preface

The reaction of those who take the time to read this writing will cross a broad spectrum of emotion and intelligence. It shall meet prejudicial and complete rejection. It shall be skimmed and spurned. It shall be parsed and diced. It may be lauded but shall surely be lambasted. In truth, it is but one man's attempt to search out the intent of inspired writings. The subject matter is not new, but to those intensely interested in the body of Christ and truth, it might prove thought provoking if nothing else.

This writing is not intended to create dogma or creed in an already dogmatic and creedal- crowded religious landscape. This writer understands and tries to respect the absolute authority of God-breathed words. There is a difference between those words and what I *THINK* those words say. They, (God-breathed words) and they alone should be the literary test tube that determines truth or fiction. I humbly beg you to be of the Berean spirit!

Since I am sure the depths of the subject matter will not been plumbed and all questions not sufficiently answered, this writers e-mail is tmbounds@msn.com. Any discussion is welcomed.

Don Bounds

Contents

Historical Background

No human writing occurs in a vacuum. Whether expositional or historical in nature, it is impossible to completely remove human perspective from that writing. Since this writer will not be able to escape that reality, perhaps the best place to start is the background of this writer. Some insight on my spiritual underpinning will help to understand my "Journey to Fellowship"

I believe in objective truth! Objective truth is facts stripped of all extraneous garnishments of a self-serving nature. Objective truth is facts void of prejudice and presupposition. Religiously, objective truth is the inerrant word of God. Therefore, <u>truth is only that which can be established by the **Word of God!**</u>

The background information supplied in this preface to this study is my remembrance of events. They are not intended to establish truth. But they will supply the historical landscape from which my thoughts and studies have grown. And perhaps, to an even larger degree, my motivation to commit them to the written word.

Those of my contemporaries who read this may or may not have similar recollections. Whatever the case, these historical events will not add to, or detract from, the objective truth of the scriptures.

Whether good or bad, some of my earliest memories of the church involved trouble and controversy. My mother was reared in the church but my father had strong Baptist roots. (their formative years being the 1930s and 40s) My father became a Christian in the mid 1940s. He was led to Jesus by a man who would not let my father escape from the words of the Bible. **And** what those words meant! (baptize=emersion) He was baptized into Christ, but immediately my mother and father became involved in "worship" using two cups.

Just after I was born, my parents moved the family (me and my older brother) to another city. There we began "worshipping" with a congregation of people who embraced the same form of worship as the congregation we left. It was at this congregation that I begin to have memories of what it was like to grow up "in the church". Even though "the church" was involved in what I hold today to be false worship practices.

1

The first controversy my young parents faced was the "night communion" issue. Because of my age, I have very sketchy first hand knowledge of the controversy. But, in a nutshell, the problem was advanced by servicemen (military service still an issue) who could not attend when "the table" was set. The table was allowed to remain "set" so that those attending Sunday evening could "have communion". The "cup issue" was not in view at this time. As is the case when religion, truth, and convictions collide, the controversy waxed "hot". The issue hinged on the word "communion". The fact that the word communion entailed participation of the body created a dilemma for the "night communion" faction. Either another "body" (church) was created who had communion with God, or there was no communion existant between those who did not "participate" with the other in the "communion" of the body and blood of Christ. To authoritatively define a word of the scriptures as demanding certain action, then do other than the word demands, defies not man, but God!

My parents, as well as several other families, refused to participate in worship they found to be in contradiction with the word of God. Even though they were still, at this time, using two cups, a move to insure worship "in truth" was made. Those families began worshipping house to house or in a funeral chapel for some time.

At this point in the narrative, I think it fitting to entertain some questions and perhaps make some comments. For one to claim "sincerity" and die "in error" has to be biblically impossible, or, we have misused the word "sincere" or "in error". 2 Peter 3:9 states God is not willing that **any** should perish. John 8:32 "Ye **shall know** the truth and the truth shall set you free." "**Seek** and ye **shall** find! Cornelius was a "sincere and devout" man who was lost. To insure the inerrant quality of these scriptures, God sent Peter to Cornelius. He sent Philip to the eunuch. God has **never** made a way for false worshippers to **be right.** But God has always made a way for "sincere worshippers" to **get right!** Truly "sincere worshippers" are the Corneliuses and eunuchs of our world who only need a "guide". (preacher/teacher/study) John 4:24 says "They that worship [God] **must** worship in spirit and in truth" Therefore, regardless of the spirituality and "sincerity" of my mother, father, and those with them, they were not worshipping "in truth"! Thankfully, by God's mercy and providence, a "Philip" was on the way!

2

Not too many months later, two gospel preachers (two "Philips") stopped to "discuss" a "new" doctrine that had been brought to my mother and father's attention. They (those who believed like the two gospel preachers) were referred to in hostile circles as "the one cuppers" or "anti brethren". Such "labels" are not always welcome, if used as ridicule, but generally serve to point out what appears to be the doctrinal keystone of that faction, sect, or splinter group. Since participation in any worship other than that which the Lord has specified, (true worship) "two cup" (or any deviation from the pattern) worship constitutes false worship. Some sins (or doctrinal differences) will not, of necessity, involve the whole congregation. The "cup" issue is a corporate worship issue that demands participation. My parents, and those with them were convinced they could not "truly" worship where the Bible pattern of worship was not followed.

The visible body of Christ, they concluded, (and I believe still stands) had specific identifiable characteristics as described and defined by the New Testament.

The New Testament Church on earth…

> Contains all the saved… Acts 2:47
> …but not <u>only</u> the saved   Matt 13:41 Matt 13:47ff
> Assembled together-----Heb 10:25, 1Cor 14:23
> On a particular day….Acts 20:7
> Must worship in spirit and in truth…. John 4:24
> Is governed **only** by the New Testament.. Heb 8:8, Heb 8:13
> Has no earthly authority or head…. Col 1:18, Rev1:11ff,
>   Eph 5:23ff

The above-mentioned points may have many sub topics, but either these things visably identify the New Testament church or we have no idea on earth what it looks like, who it is, or how it exists! The scriptures previously cited in this paragraph provide us the basis for the superstructure of the New Testament church. That was the conclusion then, as well as now!

The cup controversy

The cup issue came close on the heels of the "night communion" fray. Consequently, many of the "brothers" involved in the first discussions were also involved in this "new" doctrinal issue. It was a time when brethren showed by actions, that the issues at hand were of grave importance. It was a time when most of the brethren had less materially, but didn't seem to mind 1&2 AM "studies". No one seemed to want to "give up" on the others. Some times the discussions went on longer, and were more "boring" than my young mind could endure. But on many occasions, I could be carried along by the excitement of the moment when a new "Goliath" would show himself and taunt the "truth". Before long, I was able, even as a youth to understand the salient points. I would anxiously wait for the "David" of the occasion to turn to flight an often brazen and brash attack on the unassailable truths of the Bible! I watched and listened night after night and month after month as men from every educational echelon stepped out a slippery (and sometimes slimy) premise, which could not be supported by the book (the New Testament) they professed to know and follow.

John was an oft-quoted character. "Ye shall know the truth and the truth shall set you free"! But for many, they **knew** the truth and the truth made them mad! (Not much has changed, has it?) Many misguided "prophets" and deceived souls were made to stumble and search in vain for words to defend the indefensible. When the arguments of those who assailed the truth could not be reinforced, their voices would become louder and more strident. Some even resorting to character attacks, name calling, and other antics designed to side-track the discussion. Trying in vain to dishearten those who patiently used the scriptures as a shield and an instrument to pierce the hearts of sincere listeners.

The "cup" issue remained for some time, a major controversy for the church. (In some places, still is today) Yet 50+ years later, the bulwarks of the scriptures remain firm and sure on this issue. Today, 2005, men who claim an even greater degree of secular education still try to explain away and/or deny the simplicity of "the cup". Today I still get a "tingle" (nothing religious, just a victorious emotion) when the Lord's spiritual "Davids" cause to fall like "big timber" the modern day "Goliaths"! In so doing, God's people are empowered and encouraged to press the battle! In these spiritual battles, people are able to see the "enemy" turned to flight by God's immutable word!!

Divorce and Remarriage

By the latter years of the 1950s, the urgency of the "cup" issue had begun to subside. The battle raged on (and still does) but "the front" was beyond us. Yet almost before our spiritual feet were firmly planted on the communion, another issue is brought to the forefront of the battle. This would be an issue that would divide the camp of the "true worshippers". This issue would also divide brothers, (flesh and spirit) congregations, and families and send shockwaves that are still being reckoned with today. **Divorce and remarriage!**

The issues and events of this "division" are much clearer to me than the previous forays into controversy. I was not old enough to be a participant in these events, but old enough and interested enough to observe and listen with considerable more knowledge of the scriptures. Many who were on the "front line" of this battle have passed on. Sadly enough, battles cannot be re-fought, just studied. As has been oft quoted, "Those who do not study history are doomed to repeat it". Brethren, are **we** doomed to repeat the mistakes of yesteryear? Are we still in the finger pointing parade?

The late 1950s. As is still the case, the "traveling preachers" introduce many "new" subjects to the brotherhood. This was the case at our home congregation. I know, by the scriptures, that the subject of divorce and remarriage was not new. The controversy has raged for centuries. Yet different teaching and new discussion brought this volatile subject "front and center". "Battle lines" were drawn, and the church and our family were, once again, "at war". Or so it seemed.

Time, nor experience has not changed church controversies. Preachers have preeminently played a role. Our home congregation was introduced to the idea of "no exception", first by a preacher from Texas, followed up by one from Missouri. All previous teaching and discussion had embraced the "exceptive" clause of Matthew 19:9 as applying today. A "choice" on this issue simply had not been entertained, much less studied. Now, heresy was among us!

In my experience with controversy, there are several things that work against finding objective truth.

1. Presupposition---- ignore the facts
2. Prejudice----mind closed

5

3. Emotional issues--- ego or personal involvement
4. Family pressure--- family relationships at risk
5. Implications--- what this issue demands **I** do

As the marriage issue washed (in some cases "exploded" would fit better) over the brotherhood, some or all of the above-mentioned factors made themselves known in congregations all over the nation. The divorce rate was not as high then as now, but substantial enough for the problem to involve most families. If not immediate families, certainly aunts, uncles, cousins, etc. The implications of change on this issue were hard to entertain. Implementation would be daunting to say the least. Catastrophic and heartbreaking for too many!

For some time there was open discussion of the scriptures involved in this controversy. There was no "clear-cut" division on this issue. But as time wore on, egos and emotions began to play a role as congregations started to divide. One Lord's day at the congregation where we assembled there were "50-60", the next "35-45". As is the case in most Bible disagreements, a common phrase came to the forefront. "Test of fellowship" People were asked if they made their stance on the D&R issue a "test of fellowship". **OR** Would you still worship with someone who disagrees on that issue. There were many who "took a stand" on D&R but did not make the subject "a test of fellowship". Initially, most (if not all where we worshipped) of the divisions that occurred involved those in a D&R condition or those who simply didn't want to hear the "no exception" doctrine taught. I **never** knew of a single instance of disciplinary action being taken. ("disfellowshipping", as it's called) People just stopped worshipping together.

The preachers

The next stage of the "great divide" followed closely on the heels of the first. Preachers were called. There was a short time in which preachers were allowed to "fence ride" (not publicly state their position) on the issue. But before long, word was circulated ("the grapevine") as to what position one held. One became known in opposing camps as a "no divorce preacher" (one who did not hold to the exceptive clause) or a "divorce preacher" (one who held to the exceptive clause). Pressure was put on preachers to "take a stand". This did not only involve deciding what one thought the scriptures taught, but much more! Some congregations were advised to "cut off" (have nothing to do with) other congregations who believed different, or had used preachers who held an opposing view.

Sadly enough, this same or similar scenario is still being played out today. Just on different issues.

It appears at this point, the whole focus of the controversy took on a new light. Even though there had been no biblical severance of these different groups of people, the fray had evolved into a "them against us" confrontation! If a preacher was used at a congregation of one persuasion, he was generally "blackballed" at all the congregations who took the opposing view. The congregations of the brotherhood, at times lead (not on the surface) by influential preachers, became embroiled in a spiritual "donnybrook" that has not subsided to this day!

This division of brothers cannot be wholly attributed to personality clashes. The issue was, and is very real. The division has not been perpetrated by just one side of this controversy. There is plenty of blame to go around.

The chasm created by the disagreement over the D&R issue is deep and wide. The communication that precipitated the "great divide" has all but ceased. Oh sure, we still "preach to the choir" on the evils of D&R. But it appears to me that the overriding mission of the church (to seek and save the lost) has been drowned in the cacophony of a spiritual "Hatfields and McCoys" war that has spanned over three generations!

Today (2005), aside from the central issue, if one dares to suggest that we might be right on issue but wrong on procedure, one may be ostracized by the others in his/her "group". Apparently, even the suggestion that one of the "pioneers" of this division may have made an "honest" mistake in the handling of matters is considered "spiritual treason". Any honest evaluation of current truths must not tread on, or impugn the elders (preachers) of yesteryear! Brothers! To judge the motives and the eternal destiny of those men and women is beyond our realm and authority! But to ignore what the scriptures reveal to us today amounts to spiritual suicide!! Our handling of the revealed truth of the scriptures today shall not change the eternal destiny of our forefathers! Our failing to act on revealed truth (not miraculous, but revealed by study) does not uphold the faith of our fathers. Our acting on revealed truth makes their struggles **more** significant. They had the courage to step out and embrace what they understood to be true. May God grant that spirit to remain in us!

Over the next 2-5 years, the church as I knew it was separated into two fairly distinct "camps". Almost all regular communication and discussion ceased, except for sporadic verbal "skirmishes" in some places. The term, "test of fellowship", was used on a regular basis, but no meaningful conclusions were reached on how this term should be used or practiced in the brotherhood. In general, the only thing both "camps" came to practice with increasing regularity was **"leave them alone"**! Even though there is **no** Biblical precedent on inter-congregational discipline, the ostracizing of whole congregations followed (to some degree) the Biblical precedent for purging individual immorality from a single congregation. That unscriptural and archaic practice is overtly or covertly in place today.

It was my perception at that time, while D&R was central to the controversy, in general terms, I (and my family and others of the "no exception" persuasion) believed there to be a "conservative/liberal" mindset that ran roughly parallel to the D&R controversy. In retrospect, I (we) came to view the exception brethren as more "worldly". By the way this "division" took place and was being handled, it was a small step for me (a youngster) to see "divorce & remarriage = liberal = worldly = lost = let them alone". Conversely, "no exception = conservative = Godly = safe = fellowship". From my limited-view vantage point, the "exception" congregations **seemed** to have more "worldliness" problems. And the wider the "chasm of non-communication" and association widened, the easier it became to think those things true. This appeared to re-enforce the aforementioned equation that leads one to the "leave them alone" mind-set. "Worldliness" was roughly defined by attendance and/or participation in organized sports, racing events, bobbed hair on women, make-up, women's slacks, TV, movies, dancing etc. Even though these did not become divisive at the time, this was "the lay of the land" from my vantage point.

I do not remember **any** in-depth discussion on what our responsibility and long-term relationship with the other congregations might entail. I do remember that the evils of D&R were taught often and became a "staple" at every gospel meeting. (not saying this was bad, just the reality)

The "let them alone" stance appeared to take hold on both "sides". "Fence-riding" and "crossing the line" (worshipping or preaching) would place some preachers in danger of being "cancelled". (having a meeting called off) It was at this point that preachers were denied access to some congregations. Some by not being called, some by not being willing to go certain places, others being "threatened" with "consequences" if they went. There was never a Biblical precedent cited. The scriptures that deal explicitly with individual wrongdoers within a congregation and other misguided "scriptural missiles" were the only things offered as justification for what was taking place.

And so..... another "division" is spawned **in** the body of Christ. This time without an issue that would change the elements of worship. (mech. instr., cups, ss, etc) One Sunday, we were worshipping together, the next, there were two congregations. At times emotions ran high and most casual associations stopped from both "camps". There was some meaningful dialogue, but most deteriorated into a "fault-finding, finger-pointing" session about who aught to bear responsibility for the "division". Hasn't stopped yet! Even though roughly half (or more) of those involved have passed on.

But alas!! This was not to be the division to end all division!

By the mid 60s, the D&R controversy would fade into the background. This is not to say it became of no consequence, but the chasm of non-communication became so wide, hope of resolution faded. My family's (and myself) spiritual feet were firmly planted in "no exception" ("conservative") real estate. The fact that the majority of the brotherhood appeared to go the other way did not shake our faith in what we understood to be "the truth". In fact there was a mindset born of this fact that would allow us to remain steadfast throughout yet another fast approaching storm cloud of controversy, division, and heartbreak. When disparity in numbers (so few) were pointed out, we would rest secure in the scripture's assurance that there would "only be a few". Noah--- only eight saved. We were sincere, we were conservative, we tried to be Godly, we wanted to be safe, we were obviously the few, therefore, we had to be "right"! Not good logic but true. The scripture, "Come out from among them and be ye separate", seemed to be the mantra of the day. Even though in application, it really didn't matter whether you came out or "they" went out. The operative word was "separate".

In the political arena, there was the great debate concerning "separate but equal" schools. Even though the D&R congregations were now separate and always referred to as the church of Christ and brothers, they were not viewed as equal. Most of those we associated with at the time began to paint the "exception" brethren with a broad brush. They were "liberal, loose, lax, worldly and believed in **ADULTERY! (Not true, but the way they were painted. And still are.)** Even though we would begin to see that all these brothers and sisters did not embrace all these elements, some not even embracing the exception, the prevailing rule was "leave them alone". That is the prevailing guide to this day. Both "camps"!! (with few exceptions)

This narrative can no longer follow the next 40+ years with the "exception" brethren because the "leave them alone" policy (it was/is a "brotherhood policy") was "enforced". Any one who dared "cross the line" was branded "weak on fellowship" or would not be used at many congregations. Or the much dreaded (and little understood) "heretic" was marched out like a club to keep some "in place".

Many of these ideas and actions I could never make "dovetail" with the scriptures being quoted to justify them. But as a young man, I never felt qualified to dispute with the more "seasoned" brothers. Because of this and our own lack of study or ignorance, the misconceptions and misuse of scripture during this period will allow my family and I, (and many others as well) to continue down a wrong road for many years to come.

It would be in the next few years that my own personal beliefs would begin to solidify. That is not to say that these beliefs would be born of my own in-depth studies. But, as is the case with most people, my faith was based largely on my parental input and lots of 'preachin' .The background of my parents has already been mentioned in this narrative. Their desire to know "the truth", serve the Lord, or their devotion to the church, I never doubted. (then or now) Yet none of these qualities immunized us against the next divisive onslaught at hand. The above-mentioned points would remain the guideposts for my family in next few years of turmoil.

The Adornment Upheaval

Even before the D&R controversy had "cooled", a "new issue" burst with fury on the brotherhood. (at least the part of the brotherhood **we** thought was left) The "gold" or "adornment" (1 Tim 2:9) issue had arrived. While this subject would be taught among the "exception brethren", it would never take on the divisiveness that occurred among those we were most acquainted with. As is the case with all scriptures, 1 Tim. 2:9 was not "new". The "powerhouse" preachers in previous years had "lowered the boom" on shorts, blue jeans, peddle-pushers, etc. on women. This sinful conduct (along with many others) was portrayed as a sure reservation in an eternal hell!! But the question was posed: "Why only preach half of that verse?" For those who wanted "the whole truth and nothing but the truth", this seemed a legitimate question? Several brothers, (my dad included) began to publicly preach the negative side of 1 Tim. 2:9.

On the outset, I do not think any of these brothers understood how volatile and divisive this subject would prove to be. I can still remember my personal underestimation of the issue. I was raised with the mindset that eternity was long and Christians should "make their calling and election sure". I was just certain no one would parlay "eternal life" for **ANY** gold band! How wrong could I be?

In the beginning, the prohibition of the things mentioned in 1 Tim. 2:9 was discussed as pertaining to women only. But the hue and cry of some women became so shrill and clamorous because the men were not involved in the prohibition, it almost seemed there would be a "mutiny" in places. In my opinion, this led to an early error that is still given credibility today. Because some women more or less said, "If the men don't have to stop wearing it, (gold, etc.) neither should we". Most men (my dad included) decided to "set the example" for the women. While the willingness of some to just "take it off" (rings, watches, tie tacks, buttons, purses, ribbons, deodorant and any thing else someone wanted to use to make the position seem "extreme" and untenable) was admirable, it would soon become obvious that all the demands to "take it off" was not born of sincerity. But nevertheless, 1 Tim. 2:9 was equally applied to men and women alike. What a mistake!

Now any preacher who stood to preach the negative of 1 Tim 2:9 as it is written, dared not have so much as a brass button on his blazer. Any watch would have to be of the pocket variety, and that with a "leather chain". Or risk the label of "hypocrite". In spite of the willingness of some men to give up anything some thought was a "stumbling block", or for the "sake of peace", division was not to be averted.

Fueled by some of the same thought processes that had given us the D&R debacle, we were well on the way to the **FOURTH** major split in my short life! (I call this major because of the number involved, but there were others as well. Just not as well publicized.) I was beginning to think that a modern day "Noah and his family" **would** be all that was left!! **Literally!**

"Come out from among them and be ye **separate**" seemed once again to be the cry where the issue erupted and exploded! Context of this scripture never came into full view. But the words stated what a lot of people seemed intent on doing. Separate! So now we were a part of the " no night communion, one cup, no divorce, no gold, church of Christ"! (Try to put that on a sign.)

In this issue (probably the others as well) there were those who accepted the "no gold" view, but had grave concerns about another "division". No one denied that there were a "lot of good people" seemingly "left behind". Some denied that the "not" of 1Tim 2:9 is a negation. Some could not come to a definite conclusion. Some a mixture of various interpretations, but many of those "choking" on the idea that differences on every issue now meant more separation of brothers and sisters.

Scriptures like Amos 3:3. "Can two walk together, except they be agreed?" This text has been claimed by most sects in every "division" the church has faced! But when observing the application, it (Amos 3:3) was only applied to the disagreement at hand. When other points of disagreement were pointed out, they were made to be not so "weighty". Yet by my thinking, **who** was defining "weighty"? To those whose had lived through and struggled with the D&R issue, **that** was the greater matter. Now there were some who thought 1 Tim. 2:9 must be taught with at least the regularity of baptism, possibly more! And for a while (actually a long while) the biggest crowd during a meeting **now** would be when the "adornment issue" was taught. Even though now only "the choir" was present.

But once again the "let them alone" stance was being applied, and most of these sermons were just reinforcing "the faithful". For now those of us who held to the negation of 1 Tim 2:9, were not allowed to teach or even participate in a service where those opposing the position were in charge. We also took the position that those "who do not hear us (not the apostles, but US!) have not the spirit of truth". Therefore the teacher prohibition was not a one-way street But, as with Amos 3:3, the disparity of application to selected issues was obvious, but "papered over by our tunnel vision". Our "tunnel vision" having been created by other scriptures that were allowed to take precedence. Like 2Cor 2:6. Come out from among them and be ye separate! The context of these misapplied texts were not discussed much. But "be ye separate" seemed to have been nailed down! 2Thes. 3:6 "Withdraw yourselves from **every brother that walketh disorderly".** This was never practiced uniformly except toward those who "**believed** in the wearing of gold". I never knew of a single person withdrawn from on this issue.

1 John 1:7 "If we walk in the light as he is in the light, we have fellowship one with one another…….". "Walking in the light" was generally interpreted as having the truth and the whole truth! If "light" in 1 John 1:7 is to be equated with truth, then "as he is in the light" indicated **ALL** the truth. To us at the time, our position epitomized **all** the truth. At least all the truth that was important. Ludicrous but true.

In retrospect, this appears to be an arrogant position. The irony of the position is that some of the seemingly most sincere, honest, humble people held to this interpretation. While the whole gamut of human emotions (joy, sorrow, happiness, malice, hatred, etc) were experienced by those of this persuasion, I could not ascribe arrogance to their motives in pursuing this course. This only points up the results of a faulty premise used to support other interpretations. It points out the results of following without sufficiently investigating the ideas, applications, and interpretations of those who have preceded us. "The truth invites inspection!" That includes that which we have accepted for one year or fifty years! God's word standeth sure!

By the early to mid 70s, the "dust" from the ravages of the latest brotherhood dispute had begun to settle. This may sound like an improvement, but in actuality, things would get worse before better.

13

Now there would be other "groups" of Christians "walled off" from us. The spiritual "iron curtain" of non-association and non-communication had been extended beyond the "exception" brethren. It now included the "gold" brethren as well. I cannot speak concerning what most in those two "groups" were taught as far as association and communication with us. I can speak with authority concerning what **we** were taught! **Have no fellowship with the unfruitful works of darkness, but rather reprove them!** I can also speak with authority concerning what was practiced in **BOTH** "camps". "Leave them alone!" And alone we were. With this scripture misused (and a few others), we were entering 30+ years of a spiritual "cold war"! Even though I don't know what the other groups were taught, I know how most acted! We **ALL (both "camps")** acted as if fellowship had been severed.

In the 45 years spanning both of these last two splits, there was only **one** occasion when we (my family or the congregation we worshiped with) were approached to try to work on our disagreements. That one occasion was over 20 years ago (early 80s) with the exception brethren! This is a sad testimony for two groups of Christians who have heard countless sermons on loving the brethren and Jonah. John 13:34-35 should cause a collective shudder to pass through the brotherhood! **"A new commandment I give unto you, that ye love one another; as I have loved you, that ye also love one another. By this shall all men know that ye are my disciples, if ye have love one to another"**

But in spite of our knowledge of this both parties were willing to "write the other off" for 35-45 years. Oh sure, there were a few individual "skirmishes" and preachers taking a few "potshots" and "side swipes" at the issue. The "church journals" would "fire a salvo" once in a while. Since these journals only print one side of an issue, meaningful dialogue and discussion was never possible. It's always been difficult to determine what came first, the divisions or the papers.

In the 30+ years of the "gold cold war" there never seemed to be a shortage of problems or issues to occupy our minds or those of the Christians we were associated with. Some seemingly serious, others not so much so.

After a few years, the division over the negation in 1Tim2:9 seemed to pass the pinnacle of the controversy. But still, there were many issues which threatened to shiver a much smaller "stick" to "splinters".

During this period (80s-90s), "family churches" seemed in vogue. No one seemed to understand that the scriptures used to "withdraw from or disfellowship" the "exception" and "gold" brethren could be used to withdraw from brethren who disagreed on **any** subject! BUT ALAS! **If** the scriptures used to perpetrate and perpetuate the division of the last 45 years were applied equally and impartially, the church now would be splintered into single- family churches! In many families' misplaced zeal and the quest for truth, that's exactly what happened! Actually, if complete impartial application of scripture (as we understood it at the time) had been allowed to rule, many husbands and wives would have no longer have been able to worship together. Strangely enough, (or not so strangely) at the blood family level, folks seemed to be a great deal more "tolerant" in the absolute application (or lack thereof) of scripture. Seemed like love began to play a part......or something.

Throughout the timeframe of the division and problems discussed here, and in particular the last 30 years or so, there always seemed to be a central issue that evolved or led to another issue more "grisly" than the first. Maybe the word is "grizzled" or "knotty". I'm speaking of the "fellowship issue". Invariably, most of the long term difficulty and dissension made this topic as "hot" as the one that ignited the discussion. When one particular line of thought or reasoning began to be advanced, those opposing would try to make the issue "a test of fellowship"! When the "test of fellowship" subject would arise, one of two things usually happened. No. 1 Brethren divided. Or No. 2 Everybody got real quiet. "Real quiet" seemed always to satisfy one party if not both! Brothers and sisters talked about "the weather", or they didn't talk at all! Non-communication can hide a multitude of diversity. If one does not communicate, any number of differences may co-exist. If one clearly defines a belief (even if not practiced) there may be serious consequences! Not in the best interest of the pursuit of truth. But the reality.

Most Christians' desire to know and understand the truth was stifled by fear. At some church gatherings, fear or uneasiness that some one might bring up the wrong subject would be almost palpable. I always thought this strange of people who supposedly placed a premium on the truth and love. Most advocated a desire and need to know more truth but when a view different from their own or the "accepted" (traditional) church (party?) view was presented, the occasion might move quickly from conversation to irritation, to malice, to "disfellowshipping", and points in between!

No wonder the world views the church to be as sectarian as almost any other religious body. No wonder we've left a trail of wayward young people who are as confused as the world on unity. No wonder we are concerned in places as to whether the church will be able to perpetuate itself, (by marriage "in the Lord") much less, convert the world!

In the 90s, the facts stated began to weigh more heavily on my mind. In fact, in a conversation with my father on this issue, I made the statement to him that I thought the course being pursued was "taking us down a dead end alley". Because he could not see a legitimate way out, he did not agree. I, as well, was still unable to see a course that provided solid scriptural footing. My own struggle to get a grip on these issues would go on a few more years. (Some will say I still don't have a "grip" or "a clue"! But let's reason together!)

Even though some congregations or individuals began to associate and try to "work with" some of the "gold" brethren prior to 2001-2002, in general, there was little communication. About this time there seemed to be a renewed interest (origin unknown) in "working with one another" again. Since most felt that fellowship did **not** exist between the two groups, something would have to be done to bridge the chasm of "non-fellowship". At a time when disintegration seemed a greater possibility than unity, meaningful dialogue was welcomed.

There possibly was much more discussion than I was aware of, but this narrative is representative of this writer's perspective. I had conversation with some brothers who indicated dialogue had been opened up between the "gold/no-gold" factions. There appeared to be a desire to "restore fellowship" between the "gold fellowship" and us, the "no-gold fellowship". There may have been other brothers involved, but only three brothers from one congregation (no-gold), and one brother from a "gold" congregation were the only people mentioned in this "fellowship restoration" effort. The "gold" brother involved in this effort was the same brother who the three brothers ("no-gold") had "labeled" a false teacher for many years. They refused to allow him to take part and warned others of his status (This is usually the way "non-fellowshipped" brothers are handled. Some never being told why, or the congregation advised on that preacher's error.) This is the same brother who had written concerning his thoughts on the "restoration of fellowship" a few years before this restoration effort. He wrote, *"….. as I see it, for any of them to work with us, they* (the "no-gold brothers*) are forced to say we are right on the gold issue. They have long paralleled the not of wearing gold with the not of women preachers. Unless they give up this doctrine, they can no more work with us than the Sunday School folks."*

Whether this reflected the exact beliefs of the brethren he was associated with, I'm not certain. What I am certain of is the isolationism ("passive congregational discipline") that prevailed in both "camps" for most of 30+ long years! They (the "gold brethren") felt compelled to "bar" any one from the pulpit who left the "k-not" of 1 Tim 2:9 tied. By the same token, we (the "no-gold brethren") would not allow them so much as to lead a song, much less occupy the pulpit. For any congregation to cross that boundary, would bring "censure" from those "who seemed to be somewhat", or worse _ ISOLATION!

Even though the church recoils in horror at the mention of an earthly organization, the seeming inability of some congregational leaders to autonomously lead, makes the Lord's church look denominational at times. To the casual observer, the "repaired fellowship" over the "gold" issue would smack of an "edict from on high".

Nevertheless, after some dialogue between "the three" and "the one", it was announced (at least privately) by "the three" that "the whole truth" could now be taught at "those" congregations! This movement started at one congregation, but without explanation, the "domino effect" rippled across the brotherhood. Almost overnight, or so it seemed, we moved from 8-10 "acceptable", "faithful" places to worship, to 20 or 30. (these numbers are only approx and relative to the USA only)

If there were any amends made to allow brethren to have fellowship, who apparently had not for most of 35 years, it never became public knowledge. The only explanation given this writer was that now the "gold" brothers would allow the "whole truth" to be taught. Given the fact that the brother cited (4 paragraphs above) previously concerning "working with the gold brethren" would be the one who later would write of "sweet fellowship" having been restored or enjoyed. That brother, as far as I know, did not retract or repent of the stand he previously had taken. Many sisters still adorn themselves with some of the things forbidden by 1 Tim 2: 9. I believe this is indicative of a position that has not changed in belief or practice. But both "the three" ("no gold") and "the one" ("gold") now have fellowship and use one another in either's pulpit. The "no gold" brethren never made amends (at least none were made public)for labeling the "gold brother" a false teacher. The "gold brethren" never changed their mind on 1 Tim 2:9. The "gold brethren" claim the unifying factor to be the allowing of the "whole truth" to be taught in all the "gold" congregations. But now when the "no gold brethren" allow the "gold brother" in their pulpit, seems there has to be a spoken or unspoken agreement that he not teach his convictions on the "k-not" of 1 Tim 2:9. If the "no gold brethren" refuse the "gold" brother his God-given responsibility to preach what he considers "the whole truth", then the stated cause of the original division ("no gold brethren" said the "gold brethren" wouldn't let the truth be taught) is still present. The one saying the truth can't be taught has just changed parties! Or both have possibly agreed to let the other preach and make 1 Tim 2:9 of no eternal consequence. Oh what a tangled web we weave!

As all these events are unfolding concerning the repairing of the breach between the "gold brethren" and us, early on, one of the brothers (no gold) approached me with some ideas as to how the situation might be resolved. I did not agree with his assessment of why the split took place, nor did I agree with his solution of the problem. Even though for a number of years, I had felt we had somehow strayed from the intent of the scriptures on fellowship, my own thoughts on this troubling subject was still in the embryonic stage. My objections were not based in the fact that changes were **not** needed. Changes **were** needed! And I applaud the efforts that have been made! (But that does not necessitate my agreeing with their ideas, nor in making enemies of those who disagree with me.)

Those brethren began doing what they thought to be right and I renewed with vigor my own quest to understand one of the most abused, misused, and divisive subjects troubling the church in the last 50 years. **FELLOWSHIP!!**

Moving to the Heart of the Issue

Now more than ever, the concern of **WHO,** or **Which Congregations** we may, or may not have fellowship with, is THE ISSUE!! Where may one worship the Lord "in spirit and in truth"? If this subject is not intelligently handled, we shall continue to bring shame on the Lord's body with our divisiveness.

In each of situations that have been discussed by this writer, the "fellowship issue" (issue Def.----point of contention) has always been a secondary spin-off from the original point of the problem. After the dust settles from each fray, then the ongoing question of how to interact (or not) or view those who have taken the opposing view only deepens the controversy. From my perspective today, there has been gross mishandling of disagreements in the brotherhood at the congregational level. This narrative is not to point fingers of blame or to castigate any group, but an effort to assess an ongoing problem in search of a solution. I humbly confess a role in perpetrating division that I did not cause. Yet by "parroting" the same scriptures misused by previous generations, I (and anyone who has a part) became an unwitting participant. May the Lord forgive me.

May God grant us pardon for our mistakes, and wisdom in our quest to lead the church (at whatever congregation we may serve) out of the factional quagmire of the last 50 years!! That is my prayer. Amen!

The previous thumbnail overview of the church problems from the mid 1950s thru 2005 is by no means an overview of **all** the problems that churches faced in that period, just the major ones from my perspective. The ones that carried me along in my **journey to fellowship.** For many years I consider myself to have been on a journey (at times, it seemed a mission) **not** to fellowship, but to "disfellowship"! For every disagreement on scripture seemed to have only one conclusion if I remained impartial in my application of the scriptures I used, abused, and misapplied. Separation! Division! Factions! Isolation! Non-Communication! I now resolve to have fellowship with Jesus in his body, the church. And to have fellowship with **all** who also have that same fellowship in that same body! That shall not include my participation in individual sins that may be at times present in the body of Christ No more no less.

While truth must be contended for, we must understand that the Bible provides for us a way to longsuffer with one another while we dispel the sincere ignorance and weaknesses that typify the human state!

The misuse and abuse of the following scriptures are just some of the scriptures that have contributed to the uncertainty of the "people in the pew" on the question of where (which congregations) they **MAY worship the Lord acceptably.** Read these scriptures carefully, noticing the context of each. In the following treatise on fellowship, we want to handle these scriptures and others as well. Misapplication, abuse, and contradictions run at cross purposes with 2 Tim 2:15. Study to shew thyself approved unto God, a workman that needeth not to be ashamed, **rightly dividing** the word of truth.

Misused and Abused Texts

2 Thess 3:6 Now we command you, brethren, in the name of our Lord Jesus Christ, that ye withdraw yourselves from every brother that walketh disorderly, and not after the tradition which he received of us.

2 John 9-12 Whosoever transgresseth, and abideth not in the doctrine of Christ, hath not God. He that abideth in the doctrine of Christ, he hath both the Father and the Son.
10 If there come any unto you, and bring not this doctrine, receive him not into your house, neither bid him God speed:
11 For he that biddeth him God speed is partaker of his evil deeds.

1 John 1:6-8 If we say that we have fellowship with him, and walk in darkness, we lie, and do not the truth:
7 But if we walk in the light, as he is in the light, we have fellowship one with another, and the blood of Jesus Christ his Son cleanseth us from all sin.

Rom 16:17-18 Now I beseech you, brethren, mark them which cause divisions and offences contrary to the doctrine which ye have learned; and avoid them.
18 For they that are such serve not our Lord Jesus Christ, but their own belly; and by good words and fair speeches deceive the hearts of the simple.

1 John 4:6 We are of God: he that knoweth God heareth us; he that is not of God heareth not us. Hereby know we the spirit of truth, and the spirit of error.

Titus 1:10-12 For there are many unruly and vain talkers and deceivers, specially they of the circumcision:
11 Whose mouths must be stopped, who subvert whole houses, teaching things which they ought not, for filthy lucre's sake.

Acts 17:30 And the times of this ignorance God winked at; but now commandeth all men every where to repent:

2 Cor 6:17-18 Wherefore come out from among them, and be ye separate, saith the Lord, and touch not the unclean thing; and I will receive you,

Amos 3:3 Can two walk together except they be agreed?

Most of these scriptures (and others) have been used as "hammer and wedge" to separate and segregate brothers and sisters in Christ. If these scriptures legitimately separate, then things are as they should be. If not........

It would be good if the study of fellowship could be concise. But because of the number of scriptures and "pig-trail" arguments introduced into this discussion, brevity will not be accomplished. In this study I will try to handle these and other scriptures in an affirmative fashion. However, in the interest of thoroughness, some of the most common objections will be covered.

21

Walking by the Same Rule

The Bible, according to most people is a confusing book. This is true of many who are members of the church. Over the years preachers have interpreted, pontificated, postured, and palavered. But in spite of all the talk, most people do not understand the method to our "madness". One of the reasons subjects of a controversial nature cannot be laid to rest is that most do not know, or refuse to respect the authority that has the power to end the controversy. I will try to make this exposition as respectful of authority as I know how. In the event of oversight or misapplication, communication and refutation will be expected and appreciated.

Hermeneutics--- Law of literary interpretation

My approach to the subject of fellowship is not unlike any other subject that might be scrutinized. They are the rules that govern **ANY** communication or interpretive process. Our minds process these rules every day with split-second accuracy on most occasions of casual conversations. When wrong words, wrong grammar, and "sound-bite" quotes (out of context) are employed, misunderstanding is bound to occur.

Because the Bible is the inerrant words of God, extreme caution must be exercised in how we handle those God-breathed words!

The following rules must be respected or there is not a way in the world we shall arrive at the intent of the author! (God)

1. **What do the words mean? (definitions)**
2. **What do the words say? (grammar)**
3. **Context (who, what, when?)**
4. **Application (literal-figurative?)**

These are not my rules of Biblical interpretation, but rules for the interpretation of **ANY literary work!** Understanding the word of God does not lessen or mitigate the interpretive process, but rather intensifies! Woe to those who add to or subtract from God's inspired words!!

Words mean things! A sentence (a group of words) conveys a complete thought! Context (before and after) supplies information for appropriate application.

NOTE

If a Biblical passage is interpreted to say that which the word definitions will not support, THAT INTERPRETATION IS INCOMPETENT! One cannot "tweak" the definition to accommodate an interpretation!

The infinite ability of word choice employed by the Holy Spirit to convey the thoughts of God shall stand unassailable!

The harmony of ALL scripture on ANY subject must be sought and preserved!

The law of uniform application must be respected! The scope of the Bible is worldwide in its application. Therefore all interpretations or applications must be possible for all people of every nation for all times.

Defining the term: FELLOWSHIP

When one considers the word fellowship, it is ironic that the word that denotes and implies a union or commonality, is a word that has caused (by lack of understanding) a great deal of division.

Whether one uses Strong or Thayer or others, there are three words that seem to be the common thread of definition for fellowship: **partner, partnership** or **participant.**

However there are some things that need to be clarified on the definition of fellowship. The things stated in this part of the discussion will form a premise of basic understanding that I will try to uniformly apply each time the original form of the word "fellowship" is used. Once the definition of the word is established, any interpretation that does not embrace that definition is wrong! The grammatical usage of the term MUST be respected! The word fellowship is translated from the Greek 15 times. However the term is translated from 4 Greek words.

1. Strong's 2844 koinonos   def. – a sharer
                                 Used 1 time 1Cor 10:20

2. Strong's 4790 sugkoinoneo   def. – to share in company with—i.e. co-
                                 participate
                                 Used 1 time Eph 5:11

3. Strong's 3353 metoche   def. – participant
                                 Used 1 time 2Cor. 6:14

4. Strong's 2842 koinonia   def.- partnership i.e., participation,
                                 intercourse, benefaction
                                 Used 12 times   Acts 2:42✓ 1Cor. 1:9 √
                                                 2Cor 8:4✓ Gal. 2:9 ✓
                                                 Eph. 3:9ᵀᴿ Phil. 1:5✓
                                                 Phil. 2:1✓ Phil. 3:10√
                                                 1 Jn. 1:3✓ 1 Jn. 1:3√
                                                 1 Jn. 1:6✓ 1 Jn. 1:7√

(handwritten notes in margin: Rom 15:26, 1Cor 10:16 (twice), 2Cor 9:13, Heb 13:16, 2Cor 6:14, 2Cor 13:13, Philemon 1:6)

The original Greek words are the words chosen by the Spirit to convey the message at hand. Therefore, their definitions cannot be tampered with. Of the 12 times Strong's #2842 is referenced, a slightly different form of the word is utilized. One must use the context in order to make the correct application of definition. In most instances, that will not be difficult to do.

In laying the foundation for the correct usage of fellowship, we need to look first at the one thing that has led to the improper application of the term. The major misunderstanding stems from the grammatical misuse of fellowship. Our vernacular has allowed us to use fellowship synonymously with association. While open association is an outgrowth of biblical fellowship, biblical fellowship is not equal to, nor defined as association. And vice-versa. One may have fellowship and not associate or one may associate and **not** have fellowship in the biblical sense. I may have association with those of the world. Jesus did. (Matt 5:46 etal) Therefore, we may conclude association does not always equal or include fellowship. (partnership or participant) In 1Cor 5, Paul does not command the withdrawal of fellowship, but rather the denial (withdrawal) of free association with the fornicator.

Grammatically, fellowship is a noun and does not indicate action. Fellowship is something we **have**, not something we **do! 1 Jn 1:6&7.** Brothers and sisters, this is an undeniable fact that needs to be crystal clear in our minds. This is probably the single most important fact in changing our fallacious reasoning on fellowship. Then we have gone on from this faulty premise to build an understanding that is in error.

Origin of Fellowship

For one to be able to understand any subject, the logical place to start is the beginning. For most of my life fellowship appeared to be a given. And the withdrawal of it, a right of any congregation (and sometimes any individual) to exercise. To stop this divisive and schismatic debacle, we need to explore the origin of fellowship.

Unless we have erred in our defining of the term, (partnership/ participant) becoming a partner or participant with one another is relegated on our first being made partners or participants with Christ. **1 Jn 1:7** *If we walk in the light as he is in the light, we have fellowship one with another, and the blood of Jesus Christ cleanses us from all sin.*

The question is, how may I become a partner/participant with Christ?

Phil 3:8-12 Yea doubtless, and I count all things but loss for the excellency of the knowledge of Christ Jesus my Lord: for whom I have suffered the loss of all things, and do count them but dung, that I may win Christ. 9 And be found **in Him**, not having mine own righteousness, which is of the law, but that which is through the faith of Christ, the righteousness which is of God by faith:10 That I may **know Him,** and the power of his resurrection, and the **fellowship of his suffering**, being made **conformable unto his death**;11 If by any means I might **attain** unto the resurrection of the dead.

Therefore, **knowing** Christ, being **in Christ,** being **partners/ participants** of his suffering, being made **conformable unto his death,** and **attaining unto the resurrection of the dead** is accomplished by faith. Finally culminating in our obedience to and in the act of baptism we are crucified **with Christ**, buried **with Christ** and rise to walk a new [eternal] life **in Christ**! We are now a part of God's family, dwelling in Christ's kingdom, New Jerusalem! With our contact to the blood, we are able to "slay the enmity" and have fellowship (partnership/participant) with God that was not possible from "the fall" (Eden) to the cross. This is the **ONLY** way fellowship can be established between God and man!

Congregational Fellowship?

In establishing the origin of fellowship, we must take note of some negative issues as well. Fellowship is **never used in a congregational sense! Take time to search the scriptures for yourself on this point!** The definition of the word, **fellow**-ship, as well as logic, forbids this usage of the term! There is not one reference or indication that one congregation had fellowship with another congregation in the way we have fellowship with God. If I am overlooking **that** scripture, there is certainly none that implies, commands, or instructs us in severing of any tie that exists between one congregation and another congregation! Therefore, if there is no scriptural origin of congregational fellowship and if no command or procedure to sever congregational fellowship exists, to use the term fellowship in a congregational sense is incorrect!

Test of Fellowship

During the years of my personal knowledge of the brotherhood, there has been (and still are) some "fellowship terms" bandied about which need some examination. At times it appears the brethren take hold of "catch phrases" and, because of repetitive usage, they are accepted as truth.

One of the terms used in congregational and brotherhood problems is "test of fellowship". Most commonly used when an issue is brought to the forefront of spiritual warfare. The controversy waxes hot and brethren separate from each other. Each party claiming there was no problem until "they" made "**it**" **(the subject at hand)** a " test of fellowship".

If the term, "test of fellowship" is scriptural, the scripture or scriptures need to be cited. In trying to defend this term, several scriptures are generally used. Amos 3:3. "Can two walk together except they be agreed?" Implying by its usage the impossibility of the two parties going anywhere together because of immediate or partial disagreement. The scriptures will not support the "issue of the moment" or "complete agreement" as being a "test of fellowship". So just the fact that there is a disagreement is cited as the reason brethren can no longer worship together, per Amos 3:3!! This has always seemed strange since both parties go on to worship with and claim to be "in full fellowship" (as if there is a half fellowship) with brethren or congregations who still differ on any of half dozen issues or more! Obviously, this reduces the idea of "test of fellowship" to subjective and arbitrary at best!

Amos 3:3

I believe Amos 3:3 is wrested from its divine moorings, and used as an unscriptural "wedge" to separate or perpetrate the separation of sincere, God-fearing brothers and sisters! In our quest for truth, it will be easier at times to conclude what a scripture does **NOT** mean before we may be able to understand what it **DOES** mean.

In the past, Amos 3:3 has been used (abused) to justify most of the separation of brothers and sisters that has occurred over the last 50 years, (probably longer). Yet if we had made an impartial, universal application that coincided with our selective, topical application, (i.e. "the issue" of the moment) **we could not "walk" with our own companions!!** (husbands or wives)! No two people understand all issues the same way at the same time! Brothers, when we so misuse and abuse the word of God to defend what could not otherwise be defended, is there any wonder the world, and even the people "in the pew" cannot "get a grip" on scripture issues?

If we would only stop and consider! The logic of the words of Amos 3:3 are not competent to support the misuse that has been foisted on this scripture. There are only three ways we may choose to look at this passage.

1. "Can two walk together, except they be agreed" **on everything?** Anything less than this rendering will make us subjective judges of the topics "important enough" to preclude our walk!

OR

2. "Can two walk together, except they be agreed" **to walk together?**

Normally, this is only used to support the divisive issue of the moment. i.e. Matt 19:9, wedding rings, "convenience" worship, order of worship, and a whole host of other topics most have relegated to insignificance. Many Christian folk over the years, in trying to follow the lead of "chief" brethren's use of Amos 3:3, have found themselves alone in a "family congregation". The reason being, a difference in understanding and their trying to equally apply the same scriptures used by "chief brothers" in other church related disagreements. What is generally misunderstood by these good folks, is the "chief brothers" **selective** application! What is eventually understood by these "good folks" is that the lead of the "chief brothers" does not extend to an impartial application of Amos 3:3. But far enough to "excommunicate" (and even excoriate) those unwilling to conform on an issue deemed important to them. It seems to matter not that it took 40 (or more) years for **them** to arrive at that truth. But if others don't conform today: can't walk with them! How absurd have we been?!!

Therefore, in context and preserving the laws of harmony, walking together does not require absolute unity of thought, but requires we agree to "walk". We may be disagreeing as we walk so long as the agreement to walk is preserved. We have proved that for years in the church. **Except** on some "elevated" issues.

Even though the scriptures will not support it, and logic denies it, in some minds there must be a third interpretation. This is not the one most will admit to following, but that which has overwhelmingly been practiced by the dividers of brethren.

3. "Can two walk together, except they be agreed"[**on the scriptures or topics "we/I" think are important enough?**] **!!!!!**

If the Bible supplies a definitive list of things that create the impossibility of brethren walking together, **we need that list!** (This writing is not a denial that such a list exists.) I believe the Bible "thoroughly furnishes us" to all our needs. I have used scripture to define the origin of fellowship. We are only at liberty to use scripture to define the severance of fellowship or that which makes it impossible for me to "walk" with certain brothers or sisters. **Please supply that list!!**

TEST THIS POINT!!

Exhortations in the epistles were given to speak the same things, be of the same mind, etc. But **NEVER** was a command given to separate, "disfellowship", disassociate or leave a particular congregation of the body of Christ! In fact, Corinth, a congregation riddled by division, (believing different things and following men) and complacent in immorality (fornication), is addressed in 1Cor. 1:2 as **"the church of God"** at Corinth.

However, lest you get the wrong idea, the citing of this fact is not being used to prove the acceptability of those things before God, but only to prove God does not reject the congregation because of present lack of knowledge or sinfulness.

Paul immediately begins to address the problems and offer solutions. Exhortations to repent and correct the course, is the common thread in messages to Corinth, the churches of Galatia, and the churches of Asia. (5 of 7) If Paul, Jesus, nor any of the inspired writers suggested or commanded no action toward **ANY** of these congregations, why should we do any different?

Removal of the Candlestick

I have never seen the previous point successfully challenged. (That is not to say it won't be.) But usually at this point, Rev 2:5 is brought forth. **The Church at Ephesus.**

Remember therefore from whence thou art fallen, and repent, and do the first works; or else I will come unto thee quickly, and will remove thy candlestick out of his place, except thou repent. Rev 2:5

So then action has been commanded! **Right?** Let's examine the scriptures.

Jesus first gives the reason for possible **divine** extinction. **"Because thou hast left thy first love".** In all of my years in the church (41), I have **never** heard this reason given as to why one should have nothing to do with a particular congregation. I have **never** heard one of the "chief" brothers or an influential preacher say " You might not want to go there, those brethren have left their first love"! But I have heard warnings involving almost every issue from "personal to piddling" and "major to minor". The "major and minor" held captive to subjectivism! My brothers! If the Bible does not give us a list of the "majors and the minors", whose, or what list shall we use?!!

But those who use the church at Ephesus as proof text for removal of the candlestick, proffer the question. If the candlestick can be removed, why shouldn't **WE** remove it? My response is: If **WE** are to remove the candlestick, what scripture do **WE** use for that process? Where do **WE** find the scriptural timetable for that procedure? **Where** in scripture do **WE** find the definitive list of offences that trigger that process? **Who** are the people given scriptural authority to carry out this "candlestick-removal" process? **Who** has the **authority** or the **timetable** for this action?

The fact is: **WE** have been given **NO** authority! Jesus said, "**I** will remove the candlestick." When Jesus said, " Vengeance is mine, **I** will repay", we dare not usurp His authority! Why then should we assay to remove a church (candlestick) when that action does not belong to us? When Jesus says "Be thou faithful until death and **I** will give thee a crown of life" we would not think of assuming his role. On at least **33 other occasions** in Rev. 2&3 the personal pronoun, **I,** is used. Shall we also usurp His place in all these activities as well? Consistent hermeneutics will demand that treatment. But we can't and won't! Therefore, logic **and** scripture will preclude me (or anyone other than Jesus) from participating in the "candlestick removal" process!!

The church at Ephesus cannot be used as proof-text for our removal of a congregation from the "list of the faithful" by anyone on earth!. By the same token, the church at Sardis does not give license for sin to remain unexposed and unchecked in the body of Christ. This would be a clear violation of other scriptures addressing this topic. (1Cor 5

30

etal) What the church at Sardis does point out is the ability of a few to worship acceptably and be saved, while the larger portion of the congregation has fellowship with sin and will be lost! Evidently, all the elements that make a group of people the body of Christ, were still present at Sardis. **We need to identify those elements**! More on Sardis later.

Identifying the New Testament Church

It was my belief over many years that the N. T. Church could be identified in a Biblical fashion. However, in an attempt to justify our divisive actions (This statement is not to judge or blame, but to be factual.) we have continually changed who or what the church consists of, based on our latest revelation of "truth". Each "revelation" drawing the "noose" tighter and tighter around the number of "faithful" congregations and ever expanding the specific truths (decided by "the knowing ones") to be embraced by the "faithful".

Characterizing the New Testament Church

How does the New Testament characterize the kingdom of God on earth?

The New Testament Church must:

1. Recognize Jesus as its only head and savior of the body.
2. Have no earthly head or hierarchy.
3. Recognize no operational or doctrinal authority outside the New Testament.
4. In a congregational sense, worship "in spirit and in truth".
5. Be the only body (kingdom/family/etc.) with the ability to house **ALL the saved (Christians) of all the ages, eternally!**

Therefore, where a group of people is found, who embodies these characteristics, they comprise the body (church, family, etc.) of Christ in that area. They shall remain the body of Christ until Jesus, their head, removes their candlestick! This statement begs the question! When and how is this accomplished? When you, dear reader, find that outlined by scripture, **please** share that with this writer. Until that occurs, how about we leave God's business to God? We will only be able to discern in external matters. God shall discern the internal things. God **ONLY** is able to justly judge groups of people.

Responsibility of One Congregation To Another

While I have covered in point two above concerning the "autonomy" of congregations, historically, it becomes apparent we only pay lip service to the term. What is found in scripture concerning inter-congregational relationships? The only thing remotely resembling a inter-congregational communiqué is found in Acts 15 in a dispute over the teaching of men from Judea. The heart of the issue involved justification by faith. (What one must do to be saved.) Much "disputing" took place. In the end the words of Peter and James (apostles) held sway over the discussion and all agreed to James' solution.

This situation cannot be misconstrued or bent to justify the surreptitious "edicts" that are disseminated via letters, phone calls, e-mails, bully-pulpits or "brotherhood" journals! I would encourage brethren to earnestly consider before extending this "meeting of the minds" in Acts 15 to include just any inter-congregational meetings. I know that many who read this may see this as a condemnation of the above-mentioned methods of communication. (maybe an indictment, but not condemnation necessarily) But, shall we remain in denial? Brothers, how many times have you received (or someone you know) a message in one of the aforementioned ways telling you in veiled (or not so veiled) language if you would not make the "right" choice on an issue, or a congregation, or a brother, there could or would be "consequences". How many times do you know of preachers who have told congregations, "If you brethren don't make the "right" choice in a particular matter or issue, I won't be back.". Or a congregation warned of "consequences" if they used certain teachers or preachers? And if that brother issuing the "warning" happened to be "connected" well enough, (That means influential with "chief" brethren and "chief" congregations.) and if that congregation does not defer to the "watchdog of the brotherhood", the "offending congregation" will be isolated and "branded" as "weak, worldly" and in some cases "unfaithful"! Their meetings will be "boycotted"! (This is a not so subtle way of letting "offending" congregations know that they are "out of line"!) *But we don't have a hierarchy!!*

Now brothers, some of these things may be construed as inflammatory and incendiary in nature. If this is the case, I shall not be undisturbed by the reaction. But I believe it time to lay bare some situations that have for tooooo long kept congregations from being able to function autonomously! Being able to decide what course that congregation shall pursue in faith and practice without fear of isolation or labeling! Brethren! Congregations need to be educated! Not manipulated!!!!

Paul's Reaction to Error

The Church at Corinth was riddled with problems. Division within the body, doctrinal problems, and blatant immorality! If Corinth existed today, they would surely be "branded" worldly, weak, and divisive. Or maybe "unfaithful". Preachers would openly muse on whether "it might be best" not to go there. If Corinth happened to be in an area where leisure time was enjoyed, other Christians would have avoided that congregation. Choosing to miss altogether than to sit in an assembly where sinners were present. For even a visit to Corinth would be construed as "fraternizing", "condoning", or "having fellowship", with everyone and everything that existed at Corinth! Evidently this is not what Paul thought. For Paul did not issue a warning to any other brother concerning what actions might be necessary if Corinth did not repent. Neither did he send out an "edict" or "a suggestion" that others "on vacation" might not aught to go there "until things were straightened out" The same will equally apply to the churches of Asia where false teachers were having a heyday!

What Did Paul Do?
Paul followed the command he issued to the Church at Ephesus in Eph. 5:11. <u>Have no fellowship with the unfruitful works of darkness</u> **but rather reprove them.** Paul did not violate this scripture even though, in spite of the existant problems, he addressed them as **the church at Corinth**. In spite of their problems, he intended to return to the congregation. In spite of the blatant moral degradation that was present, Paul still addressed those at Corinth as the church. Read Paul's salutation in 1Cor. 1:1-9 and see his opinion of the congregation as a

whole. He called them saints! Without the repentance of the guilty, his return promised an even tougher apostolic message. But there is never even a **hint** of "repent or I'll warn the brotherhood about Corinth" and never come back!

Literally, Eph. 5:11 says, Do not be a participant with, or condone these sins (sinners) **BUT reprove them!** There are two things commanded in this passage. In general we have abused or misused the first and, in the main, ignored the second. "Having no fellowship" has been equated with having no association or at least forbids one worship at a congregation where some of the Corinthian problems are present. We do a lot of "preaching to the choir". (preaching to those who agree) Nothing wrong with that, but it does not fulfill the command to reprove **THEM. The guilty, the unfruitful works of darkness.** Reproof is defined as a confutation. Confute means to **overwhelm in argument.** Have we become so weak and unprepared that reproof is too difficult to contemplate?

Today, in the church, if one is able to overwhelm in support of the traditional (status quo) beliefs of the church, he is lauded. But if one is able to overwhelm the traditional beliefs with argument difficult or impossible to refute by the inspired words, he is likely to be branded a wrangler or troublemaker or worse. When one tries to misuse or abuse the inspired words of Eph. 5 to perpetrate the labeling of a troubled congregation as "unfaithful" and proceed to wall them off from as many brethren as possible, **WHO** is the wrangler? The one guilty of the unlawful striving is the one who finds oneself crossways with the words of the scriptures! (Some of these terms will be discussed at length under other headings)

Association and Fellowship

Association can take place on different levels. One may have a business partner where association and fellowship, by definition, are hard to separate. Because of proximity, one may associate with a fellow-employee and work toward the same goal for the same person or business. Yet in spite of the mutual endeavors of both, it could not be rightfully concluded that you agree with, or endorse **EVERYTHING** your fellow employees might be doing or saying!

Therefore, by scripture (Matt 9:10-13), by definition, and logic, association may take place in some cases without fellowship being present. The root of the word fellowship is koinos. Literally meaning common. It is the same root from which comes the word "communion". When Christians have communion, they find commonality (joint participation) in the body and blood of Christ. (NOTE: The commonality is not in the assembly. To be discussed later in this writing.)

If then, when we have communion, we know there is a reveler (car races, ball games, or other entertainment fueled by alcohol) in the next seat who also eats the bread and drinks the fruit of the vine, have you by association or communion became a reveler? Because you have shared in common with that person the bread and cup, should you be considered as "having fellowship" with reveling? That reasoning is preposterous! The scriptural use of the words fellowship and communion will not allow that interpretation!!

This writer would call your attention to the definition once more. FELLOWSHIP=Partnership or Co-participant. Therefore to merely sit in a worship service with sinners or even to "have communion" in the presence of sinners, (self-condemned eat and drink damnation to THEMSELVES) does **not** in essence transfer the guilt of one to all the communicants. Sin is not passed in communion like a communicable disease!

But the objection is quickly raised. "But what if you know of the sin and do nothing about it"? Please read on.

Authority and Responsibility

Every member of a congregation is given responsibility over some things. But every man's (or woman's) responsibility before God stops at exactly the place that God takes away or limits one's authority to act! For example. If a man directs his home in an unacceptable fashion, in judgment, shall the woman bear equal condemnation? After all she was a participant and partner in the home and in the marriage! Shall women in the congregation be held responsible for things not within

35

their God-given power to control or change? Shall the young, or those not empowered, be held responsible by God for things they have no control over? Not a Chance! *Note: This will be covered in more depth in the segment on **contribution and distribution**.

The Church at Sardis

The church at Sardis can no more be used as justification for a dead or dying church any more than Laodicea can be cited as desirable in their blind and puffed up condition. One cannot "run to the church at Sardis" to justify sin in a congregation! Sardis teaches no such thing!! But these were real congregations and the words of exhortation and encouragement given by the Lord still speak volumes! If Sardis proves nothing else, it proves that the majority of a congregation may be wrong or lost, but Jesus will still save the few! He will surely do for any what he promised the "few" at Sardis!

In a congregation of vain worshippers, Sardis had a few who refused to participate in or condone the sin that pervaded the Sardis congregation. This is not to say one **must** stay at a congregation where sin is winked at or where the membership is lukewarm. But in spite of all the problems at **all** the congregations in the Bible, **not once** was anyone told to switch congregations! The fact that the Bible says nothing, says it all! Not once was anyone told to "pull off" and start a "new" congregation. But the fact that today, we have more congregations started by "disputes" than evangelism, should cause us to reconsider our beliefs on fellowship and true worship! (Maybe some other topics as well.)

We have already examined the church at Ephesus and the church at Sardis. What else can we learn in regards to how Jesus (the **only** one to whom a congregation is answerable) views congregations?

The Church at Pergamos

The church at Pergamos apparently managed to exist at the epicenter of satan's activity in the first century. There was also some at Pergamos who had not denied the faith and who still respected the authority of

Jesus. But still, as a congregation, there are deficiencies extant. Pergamos has two false doctrines in the congregation. The teaching of Baalam and the teaching of the Nicolaitans. Pergamos can not be used as justification to hold the doctrine of either one. But they are another example of a congregation where error existed and was still recognized by God as the church at that location. Use of this scripture should **NOT** be construed as an attempt to make the presence of false doctrine (of any stripe) a desirable thing. Just another instance where error was present and God was still striving with them. **Would you?!**

Jesus said "Repent or **I** will come quickly and fight against **THEM** with the sword of my mouth". While we may not explicitly know what is meant by this threat, we can better know what is **not** meant **and who** the action belongs to. There is nothing in scripture to equate "fighting against them with the sword of my mouth" and His promise to Ephesus to "remove the candlestick". Unless the scriptures make those two actions synonymous, we cannot! (as in the equation of church and body. Col 1:18) If **OUR** use of the "sword of the Spirit" (the word of God) is the same as what **Jesus** would do "with the sword of [Jesus] mouth", (i.e. removing the candlestick) how shall we distinguish between rebuking or reproving and removing the candlestick? Brothers, when we use the springboard of assumption to arrive at an assertion, we will land in the quagmire of confusion! Allow the words to say what they say and go no farther! Not this text, or **any** text remote from this, gives us the authority, or any procedural grounds to do **anything** to another congregation in regards to "the candlestick"!!

The church at Thyatira

Jesus starts out with this church like the others. "I know thy works, and charity, and service and faith". Would anyone want, or be able to stand in Jesus' place to make this kind of judgment on an entire congregation? Would anyone today like to put out a definitive list of the "faithful" congregations? This would be a list of congregations where one "**could**" worship in spirit and in truth! **Who will be so bold?** Yet in spite of our example of Sardis, Pergamos and Ephesus, etc., congregations of the body of Christ are walled off, ostracized, isolated, ignored, and castigated as "unfaithful"! May I be so bold as to ask, "**faithful before whom**"? The traveling preachers? The scripture clearly states that we (all congregations) stand or fall before our own master. By what this writer observes today, if our brotherhood situation had existed in the first century, Thyatira and all four of her offending sister congregations would have been "written up" (this means specifically or anonymously censured) in the "brotherhood paper". Paul would have been warned against "fraternizing" with the churches of Galatia and Jesus would be reprimanded for allowing a "tolerance movement" to take root in Asia!

The truth is, brethren, in the first century, preachers did **not** hold sway over congregations. We have no record of a "preacher ultimatum" (the classic "if you use _____", or "if you don't change_____, I won't be back!") being issued to a single congregation! They did not pay lip service to church autonomy, then "kowtow" to the "editor/bishop" of their day. After all, it was decreed in Micah 4:2. "….the word of the Lord shall go forth from Jerusalem".

The church at Laodicea

Probably the most "taught on" of all the churches of Asia. Ostensibly as the "lukewarm" church. Yet the outward appearance belied a deeper cause. Lukewarmness was the result of congregational blindness. They thought they knew who they were, where they were, and what they were. Quite possibly the "best" congregation in Asia. In the" middle" of the Lord's will. The "model" congregation! Oh, of course they wouldn't dare verbalize that sentiment, but it exuded from their spiritual pores. If only they could have seen their arrogant, self-centered, pharisaical, complacent spirit!

Laodicea was not cited by Jesus on one doctrinal deficiency or a single morality problem! They were mechanically sound and spiritually bankrupt! Of the five unsound congregations mentioned, Laodicea today, would be the most likely to be publicly commended for their "meetings" and other manifestations of their "soundness". I would probably be among the number handing out the "kudos". Because the Bible says "Man looks on the outside but God sees everything"!

Brethren let's admit one thing. We have our hands full trying to make individual assessments at our home congregations. Why would we try to visit our own ignorance and short-sightedness on another congregation where we have no authority, therefore no responsibility!! What you see at a modern-day Laodicea, may "make you sick". But remember, that congregation is not represented as being "in **your** mouth". So don't **YOU** try to "spew them out"!

Responsibilities of Teachers and Preachers

Because of our carnality, blindness, and ignorance on fellowship, many, if not most of us would be the modern-day Jonah if called on to help one of *those* churches out! Our modern day "toe-the-party-line" preachers would tell the churches of Galatia, "You get rid of "those" teachers and I'll come preach for you". Or to Corinth, "You get rid of that fornicator (or adulterer) and I'll come preach for you". You take a stand for the truth I'll come preach for you! Brothers! If they could know what to do and what to believe without your preaching, why call you?! The "whole need not a physician"!! It's easy to preach on sectarianism when there's not a sectarian in the assembly! It's easy to preach against the pope.......when you're not in Rome! It's easy to preach the "no-exception" law....when only the "choir" is present! But when you cry out against Diana in the city of Ephesus.....there might be trouble. Even personal trouble!

Brethren, for far to long, preachers have been content to wage "guerilla" warfare. (from "the bushes") We have been content to let the "faceless" "editor/generals" launch "long-range" salvos from the relative safety of their "ivory towers" where not a chance of rebuttal exists. The preachers are preaching unity but the editorial "napalm" leaves nothing but scorched earth where "choice vine" has been planted. Nothing but chasms so deep and wide, it appears there are no girders of brotherly love strong enough to span the straits of malice and carnality that created it! When shall mature Christians be able to work with one another in open communication? When shall brotherly love, meekness, and spiritual mindedness make the division of brethren more difficult than over the last 50 years?!!

When those who have the ability and the opportunity to reach the lost, (in the church or out) won't, who shall give account? For the last 50 years, even to this very day, (2005) able men can be called to certain congregations (who **need** exhortation and reproof) to preach, and they will not go! Shame on you/us "Jonahs"! For over 50 years, able gospel preachers have been "shelved" (funds cut off, forbidden to speak or ignored) over an issue elevated to preeminence by the influential among us. Then we can be found scratching our heads as to why we don't have more qualified preachers available! More shame on us!!

Excuses for not preaching at certain congregations

They believe in _____. This blank can be filled in with several things, but the most common among those I know today is the sin of adultery. It can also be filled in with any of several of the "elevated" doctrines.

Brothers! Let's be truthful and fair in our analogies and representations, **even** of those with whom we disagree. The brethren we refer to do not believe in adultery by definition. But the disagreement revolves around what constitutes that sin. We (those of the no-exception persuasion) would be closer to agreement with most of those brethren, if we understood Matt.19:9 and Matt 5:32 to apply to us today. How can the above-mentioned excuse be used to not go and share with them, in **any** way we can, what we believe to be the truth on this (or any other) vital subject? The presence of sin or false doctrine does not of necessity draw a "line in the sand". It did not in the first century church; why now?

"Convenience worship" is another subject that could fill in the "blank" mentioned above. It is now competing for schismatic prominence among us. Over my lifetime, we have been known to fight sectarianism "tooth and tong"! But when that same spirit is among us, we don't seem to recognize it for what it is. Why? This subject is presently being used as a wedge between brethren, preachers, and congregations! In congregations where this practice is present/practiced/condoned, these brethren are labeled, excoriated, isolated, and ignored by those who would be our self-appointed "keepers of the candlesticks". Ignored by those who proclaim to have the truth on this issue, but evidently believe the mere presence of this doctrine has made true worship impossible.

40

Brethren, this decision should not be fueled by editorial dictations! Shall this cause the same rift among brothers as 1Tim. 2:9 and other "wedges"? It is not any more deserving of "church-splitting status" than 1Tim 2:9!!!!

Over the last few years, we have made great strides in laying aside our previously divisive, and anti-social attitudes regarding our understanding of 1Tim 2:9. This has not happened because of consensus in understanding on the scripture itself. I would venture to say all believe that a violation of whatever that verse prohibits or allows will cause one to be lost. But up to this point, we just cannot reach uniformity in interpretation on what has been prohibited or how much.

We have those among us in the congregations, and preachers, who hold diverse views on 1Tim 2:9, and apparently, we can walk together! **Some**, evidently believe this subject is not worth an "honorable mention". For they wear some of the things forbidden by this scripture, and never mention it from the pulpit. (If I believed it to be a subject of non-soul-condemning quality, I wouldn't take up valuable pulpit time with it either!) **Some,** feel obligated to say something, but think that the "k-not" in this scripture can be untied. **Some,** like to ignore the context, and make the verse apply to men and women alike. **Some,** trip merrily along in the text and "romp and stomp" on the positive affirmation of what women are to wear, (modest apparel, etc. These things sometimes spelled out in graphic detail!) **then** get a good case of "amnesia" on the negative side of the verse. **Some,** seem to think that if these things can be categorized as "growth sins", we can "work with", " walk with" and "fellowship with" those who do those things! **AND** "bid Godspeed" to those who would teach (public or private) what some believe will cause souls to be lost! All of these beliefs exist among us, yet we "walk together"! Brothers, we need some consistency in the application of the scriptures that allow us the privilege of "unity in diversity" on 1Tim 2:9 (and many others!!) but not on "convenience worship". **Or** that privilege cannot exist!

How have these (and maybe a few others) subjects managed to be elevated above a **HOST** of other disagreements that still exist? All congregations are bound to walk by the same scriptural rules. So we, as " people of the book" need to cite the scriptural rule that will elevate the nature of the disagreement to "church splitting" status. **WE must have scriptural authority for everything we do!**

"Adultery is one of the BIG Sins"

The above statement or a variation of it is the reason given for the 50+-year division on this issue. (with no end in sight)

***** For the Record*****

READERS! Please note the following paragraph!

Even though this writing will not deal extensively with divorce and remarriage, I feel compelled to state, with as much clarity as possible, that I **do not believe in, will teach against,** and **will not condone divorce and remarriage for any cause.** (1Cor 7 & Rom 7) **I will have no fellowship with adultery or adulterers** (Eph. 5:11) This is not stated to alienate my brothers of the exception persuasion, but only that all may understand my belief that fellowship exists by Biblical genesis, and not all differences dissolve that fellowship in Christ.

****

Now, is adultery the "church-splitting" sin? Is it the "biggest" sin? It has been publicly stated and written up in the church paper; "Adultery heads the list!" Is this absolutely true, or does it just sound good, **IF,** one wants to make adultery (and those who misunderstand or have been mislead) a "church-splitting sin?

What does the Bible say concerning the hierarchy of sin?

For one to say that sins differ is not a profound statement. In this world, different sins have different implications (results). For instance, liars shall not inherit the kingdom. Yet one may repent and straighten out the untruth. Murderers shall not inherit the kingdom. One may repent but cannot restore life! Therefore the implications of different sins are different. One may steal the companion of another (by divorce and remarriage) and correct that error. If one murders the companion of another, even though one repents, restitution cannot be made. If

42

therefore, the implications of sins supply the logic for sin hierarchy, murder must "head the list". For it cannot be undone or corrected.

But let's go a step farther. Statistics tell us an overwhelming majority of sins (crimes) are committed by people under the influence of drugs or alcohol. Those guilty of those things usually say, "If I had not been drinking/using, I would not have _____". Does this reasoning allow the sins of drunkenness and witchcraft to overtake adultery at the "head of the list"? After all, people under the influence of these things murder, steal, commit adultery, fornication, and a host of other sins! Other reasoning or logic might be employed to make a case for the superlative status of other sins. But if we do not appeal to the scriptures for our authority, the basis for our faith and practice rest on abject subjectivism! Not a good thing for those who supposedly "speak where the Bible speaks and are silent where the Bible is silent"!

Then what does the Bible say about "big" and "little" sins"?

In truth, the Bible says **nothing** concerning "big or little sins"! **But,** someone quickly objects. What about the "weightier matters of the law"? Let's examine! The Bible does clearly define sin! "Sin is a transgression of the law". (1 John 3:4) The "transgressions" ("weightier matters") of the hypocritical scribes and Pharisees in Matt. 23:23, involved things **omitted**, (judgment, mercy, faith) **NOT** sin they had committed! Jesus chided them for their setting priorities on things that **he** had not set!! Therefore, if we are going to make things (sins or anything!) big or small, should we not make sure the **Bible** has so delineated!! Therefore the division of brothers cannot be supported by the "hierarchy of sin" (big sin) argument.

Does the observation of preeminence in certain "lists" establish the "hierarchy of sins"?

To study this point, we must appeal to the laws governing hermeneutics. The law of harmony must be applied. This law is not some archaic, humanistic ranting, but that to which we have necessarily appealed to gain a clear understanding of the Bible. According to this interpretive tool, there must be harmony or uniformity of usage in order to make a precept binding. Example. On the cup issue, every time cup in the communion is referenced, only the singular form is used.

43

If the Bible writers had used the singular in one place and the plural in others, or vice-versa, one could rightfully assume the number had no significance in the commands regarding the communion. But since there **is** harmony in **every** instance on this subject, we use that harmony to exclude anything else! That is **not** the case on adultery and the lists **that** sin is included in. Therefore, while not trivializing adultery, one may not elevate it to "church-splitting status" based on the seriousness of the offence! There is no scripture to do so! That sin is to be handled scripturally within the local body. Failure to do so shall bring divine (not human!) censure on those guilty in **that** body! Rev. 2 & 3.

What if the church does NOT deal with the sin? Then what?

The first point that needs to be mentioned is one already established. We **must** operate within our personal power and responsibility in a single congregation. We **must** acknowledge our limited ability to judge other congregations. Our discernments of other congregations (as faithful or unfaithful) must be rooted in being able to identify the elements or characteristics that make a group of people the body of Christ. This is not to say that we must have our "head in the sand" concerning what we believe to be deficiencies in doctrine or practice. But the "candlestick removal" process is not our realm of operation!

****

In trying to answer all concerns brought to view by the fellowship/worship study, 1Cor. 5 is a chapter that needs to be scrutinized. It is a Biblical example of an extremely troubled and fractured congregation. It is an example of inspired solutions! It deals with extreme immorality and an apathetic membership. It is a New Testament example of purging (cleansing) illustrated with an Old Testament template (type). This chapter also introduces at least two terms that needs to be explored and understood. "Not to keep company" and "no not to eat". The understanding of these terms must be firmly rooted in objective authority, not subjective reasoning!

I will approach this segment of study with a verse-by-verse exposition. I will then use the information exposed as a further exegesis on our study of the fellowship/worship issue.

Exposition of 1 Cor. 5

Jesus, in his attempt to correct popular misconceptions of his day, in his discourse on the mount, started with, "It hath been said of them of old time....". Then went on to strip away all extraneous man-made, traditional conceptions on the topic under consideration. Even though his attempt to set the record straight made use of "God breathed words", (inspiration) man still tries to misuse and abuse **his** words to embrace his prejudice, presupposition, or a life practice they do not wish to change!

I am quite certain that this dissertation will not lay to rest all questions or controversy. However, I believe it incumbent upon all Christians to make an honest effort to dispel as much ignorance as possible. In Rom 1, God gave those people over (stopped striving with their intellect) to accept things as right that God **NEVER** intended to be right! 2Thes. 2:10 also warns of the consequences of our not having a "love of the truth". I plead with God's people everywhere to be the modern-day Bereans and receive the "engrafted word which is able to save your souls"!

Since I want this to be an exegesis, I will try to remain true to the endeavor. Some men call their verbal exercise an exegesis but instead it becomes an eisegesis. A true exegesis **extracts** the meaning of the text, while an eisegesis **injects** one's personal ideas into the text. But the Bible warns against foisting our private interpretation on "God breathed" words! 2Peter 1:20

....

NOTE: I know the following segment on hermeneutics is redundant. Yet given the importance of HOW study is accomplished, it is this writer's desire to solidify these points by the redundancy.

....

As in every endeavor to truly understand God's word , hermeneutics **MUST** play a role. If there is not a uniform method that rules our interpretive procedure, what chance do we have in understanding the word of God or being able to bring ourselves to maturity in Christ? Deciding what we believe, **then** going to the Bible to prove it, is to commit spiritual suicide.

Hermeneutics

Interpretive methods may involve more than I outline, but I will be using three basic avenues to approach the lesson at hand. These are not convoluted, hard –to-be-understood, intellectual, pinheaded ideas. This is the way we learn to converse and convey ideas on a day-to-day basis. Yet when it comes to the Bible, rather than honing our interpretive skills, we treat the words of the spirit with less respect than the people we converse with daily! To accept the Bible as the word of God and accord to it, inerrancy, is to admit that God understands language, and said **<u>EXACTLY</u>** what he meant to say. I will give the utmost attention and respect to that statement!

Interpretive Rules

1. <u>Words mean things</u>! So first, words must be defined. If we are in doubt of the intended thought conveyed by a writer, the words used must be defined by the vernacular of the writer's day. No interpretation can be considered acceptable when the definitions of the words used are not competent to support the interpretation laid forth. Whether literal or figurative the interpretation **<u>never</u>** conflicts or overruns the definition of the words used by the spirit.

2. <u>Grammar</u>. What do the words say? The arrangement (subject, verb noun, adjective, tense etc) and use of certain sequences of words allow the writer or speaker to communicate with clarity, the thought to be conveyed. In the case of the Spirit, this is done flawlessly! Man fails in appropriate word usage and syntax, but not God! God's grammar will **never** fight with the word definitions.

3. <u>Context and Application</u>. Who? What? When? Context may limit or extend the point being made. Context (scripture before and after) may allow the reader to understand exactly who was being addressed and when. Context will **never** fight with or overrun the grammar or the word definitions! Harmony of **all** scripture **must** be maintained!

State of the Congregation

In looking at the broad context of this writing by Paul to the church at Corinth, one can almost be overwhelmed by the quantity and depth of problems existing at this congregation. If the apostle had not spoken, without reservation, (1Cor 4:19) of his visitation, one might assume there were no "embers" on which a spiritual breath could blow! After all, there was schism, immorality, and a host of other "problems" this congregation seemed to fall short in. I shall try to focus on the immorality problem.

Verse 1 & 2

That there was a problem at Corinth seems evident to us, the readers after the fact. But the truth is, the magnitude of the depravity was not evident to the church as a whole. Even though Paul said, "It is reported commonly (many others were aware and knowledgeable of the problem) that there is fornication among you, and such fornication as is not so much as named among the Gentiles, that one should have his father's wife." The sin of fornication is made no worse to God by its specific nature, but, as is the case today with certain sins, some immorality remains repugnant even to those outside of Christ. This was the case with the man at Corinth. Paul begins to make his case against the congregation by chiding them for condoning a sin so odious, the world (pagans) didn't even discuss it openly!

But instead of the congregation sitting in "sackcloth and ashes", (mourning) they apparently were more caught up in the party spirit Paul had already pointed out to them. Instead of understanding the malignant nature of sin unexposed and unreproved, the use of the words "puffed up" indicates a smug or satisfied feeling! Paul's rebuke goes even deeper after he chides them for being smug about the sin. When he says, "and have not rather mourned that he which hath done this deed might be taken away from among you."

Verse 3

In this verse, Paul exhibits his apostolic power and authority. We, as uninspired men, will not be able to stand in Paul's shoes in discernment of situations in congregations where we are not members. (Even though, much to the detriment of peace and unity, some do try!) That is not to say we will not be able to discern problems in a congregation . We just can't speak with Paul's apostolic authority. In this verse Paul validates that which had been commonly reported as being true.

Verse 4

The apostle in verse 4 begins to outline the solution to the blight of immorality that had manifested itself. Since Paul did not teach different things at different congregations, Paul's solution will be universally binding when that same situation is found anywhere, anytime! For those slow to hear, that includes today!

"In the name of our Lord Jesus Christ," Contrary to popular belief, this term, "in the name of" does not command or insinuate words to be said, (i.e. Matt 28:19) but means "into" (the possession of) or "by the authority of". **NOT words to be said before you start! (i.e. "In the name of the Father ,Son And the Holy Spirit") But a validation of the authority by which a thing is done.**

"When ye are gathered together" Some, in a convoluted effort to make Sunday morning (or whenever the communion is observed on first day) the only "binding" assembly, contend that the instructions of Paul can only be carried out at that assembly. I will not stray far from the text under consideration, but if it can be proven at all, the word "when" does not delineate the day in view. **AND!** Since Paul invokes or calls on the authority of Jesus to carry out his instructions on "when", to **deny** these instructions could be carried out at any other "gathering together" is to admit those "gatherings together" are not scriptural! (authorized) This study (1Cor 5) will not allow an exposition on that subject, but this text neither supports or denies exclusive Sunday action. It does say this action has the authority and power of Heaven behind it!

Verse 5

"To deliver such a one unto Satan for the destruction of the flesh, that the spirit might be saved in the day of the Lord Jesus"

The most common, simplistic rendering of this passage by most, is "disfellowship 'im"! However, "disfellowship is not a Biblical term! Neither can the concept be supported by scripture. "Rapture" is not a Biblical term, but **can** be supported by scripture. (Note: "The rapture" as outlined by sectarians cannot be supported!) Trinity is not a Biblical term but **can** be supported by scripture. Since "disfellowship" is not Biblical in word, or in practice, authorized, this must **not be** what Paul had in view with his command to "deliver such a one unto Satan…"

48

Let's look at the words "to deliver". One's initial reaction might be to place that person physically in the possession of Satan. Since that is not possible on more than one level, let's look deeper. The words, "to deliver", is Strong's #3860. Def.-- to give up or surrender.

This same Greek word is used in Rom 1:28. It is stated of the homosexuals, (and those so inclined to condone this evil) "And even as they did not like to retain God in their knowledge, God gave them over to a reprobate mind,….." When men or women, by **their continuing** ungodly actions, remove themselves from God's fellowship, the call of the spirit is lost. It is a sobering, and even frightening thought, that one might resist the call of the spirit (by not loving truth-Rom 1:28-or by being so callous to sin-1Cor. 5) so that even God will give us up to our own evil mind!

When one makes Jesus, Lord of their life, and by faith, and in obedience to him, become his brother and partner, fellowship(participation in life eternal) is established between that one and his God. Likewise, when one recognizes another who has been obedient to the same gospel, the "right hand of fellowship" (a figurative expression) is extended in recognition of that mutual life in Christ. God, who is faithful, will not fail in his agreement to save the faithful.

However, when we knowingly live (walk) in sin, as the fornicator, in 1Cor 5, we separate (break the partner ship between us and God) ourselves from God. We no longer "have fellowship" with Jesus. We break our agreement with Jesus and loose our benefaction. (eternal life) **Therefore, no one "disfellowships" another.** I, by living in sin, have severed myself from Jesus and **all** spiritual blessings! Eternal life included! Conversely, other children of God who had previously recognized a mutual partnership with Jesus, and hence, one another, **must** recognize me as one no longer a partner or participant (in life eternal). Since our fellowship(partnership) with one another is predicated first on our fellowship (participation) with God, when one breaks that "lifeline" with God, **THEY (the sinner) also have effectively severed their fellowship (partnership AND associations) with ALL whose fellowship with God remains intact!!**

SO.....

By definition, when one is "delivered" to Satan, the combined spiritual influence, constant exhortation, and close contact is withdrawn. One is stripped of his spiritual support system and allowed, without restraint, to live in, or search out those sins destined to destroy soul and body! As the prodigal son, was "let go", and the influence and support of the "father's house" was lost, he ended up in a "pigpen of iniquity" before coming "to himself". Sometimes, "in the gutter" or "rock bottom" is the only place that allows one to look up.

One of the reasons Christians don't practice the disciplinary process is the pain involved in the action. It is difficult for the ones who carry out this process, and, as is the case with all chastisement, unpleasant to the recipient. But, the Bible is true! Afterward, it yieldeth the " peaceable fruits of righteousness".

Another reason this is not practiced is fear! Many will say, "You'll just drive people away!" But consider this. In spite of the scriptures, some say spanking children won't work. Shall we hearken unto man or God? Some are repulsed and fearful of the common communion cup! Shall our fear paralyze our obedience? As proper chastisement works on our children, so shall **proper** chastisement accomplish God's purpose in those who are exercised thereby! Fear not!

Verse 6

"Your glorying is not good. Know ye not that a little leavening will leaven the whole lump?"

Not only did these people have no thought of cleansing, but evidently felt the man was

"A-OK"!

"A little leavening leaveneth the whole lump"

The idea of leavening needs to be looked at. This is one of those "stand-by" passages oft called to condemn the issue that has been elevated to "church-splitting", or "crisis" status. But a host of other sins or wrong ideas are the recipient of "all longsuffering"! If some preachers, or the "editor/bishops", or those who "seem to be somewhat" elevate the issue, that issue will be pointed out as endangering the whole lump. (congregation) But other things can trouble a congregation(s) or

50

individual members for years! Ostensibly, without causing a problem! How can these things be?

"A little leavening leaveneth the whole lump" is a maxim or proverbial in nature. Yet a saying does not attain the status of maxim except it be universally true! Therefore my explanation of this phrase must acknowledge the absolute truth of the statement.

Some would have the word leaven to represent sin or corruption of any kind. This is not true! Matt. 13:33. "....The kingdom of heaven is like unto leaven, which a woman took and hid in three measures of meal, till the whole was leavened." Obviously, the word "leaven", may not " be painted with a broad sinful brush".

Mr. Strong defines leaven and leavened (Strong's #2219 &2220) as "causing to be hot or ferment" and Mr. Thayer of #2220, says "to mix leaven with dough". Therefore "leaven" (whatever is reckoned to ferment or "move") is the agent, and "was leavened" (the change) is the result. Leaven will not (cannot) work until mixed with the "dough". Is the nature of leaven uncontrollable? Not if identified and handled properly. Anything, intended or allowed to influence (leaven) will accomplish its purpose better when practiced covertly. Many people, who we would influence for the better, will resist if they are aware of your intent. Hense, the admonition applies. "Be wise as serpents and harmless as doves" Sin, likewise, will accomplish its ultimate goal if left undetected, unreproved, unsegregated and unpurged!

Another point in regard to "a little leaven...".

In the opening statement of this section, this passage was referenced as a "standby" scripture. I refer to it in this fashion because my brethren use it to heap condemnation on brethren who do not agree on the points of doctrine **THEY** have chosen to elevate to "church-splitting" status! Yet if another brother holds another doctrine to be of the same significance, those same brethren may judge him to be divisive, a troublemaker, a false teacher, or even a heretic! Brethren, if this maxim is true, (And it is!) just applying it to **OUR** "pet issues" like adultery, "convenience worship", and fellowship, make for bad hermeneutics and blatant subjectivity in our application of the scripture! By **common** application and usage, the scripture would read; "Know ye not brethren, that only **MY** list of leavening agents (sins) will leaven the whole lump.

The other things must be suffered with "long". This just can't be! Brothers, we **must** desist in our subjective application of scripture!!

SELECTIVE

Closed circuit to those whose feel they are God's "brotherhood purging" sickle.
(I hope this title doesn't stop all readers.)

The "whole lump" is **not** the whole brotherhood or all congregations. That is, unless there is a stated or implied connection in the scriptures between congregations. **There is <u>NOT</u> ONE!!**

There is only two ways the term, "whole lump", may be applied. To a single congregation. Or to an individual member. One needs to purge oneself and play one's legitimate role in purging the congregation where one may possess some authority. Where one has authority, one has responsibility! There are those in the brotherhood who use Paul's enumeration of the burdens of his life in 2 Cor 11. In verse 28 of that passage he concludes by saying, "Beside those things that are without, that which cometh upon me daily, the care of all the churches". That we should have care for all the churches (congregations) and "love the brotherhood" is undeniable! But that "care" does not extend to the responsibility of "labeling" or "purging" all those he may disagree with. Therefore when preachers, teachers, editors or "a chief brother" issues an ultimatum concerning who, what or when "purging" is to be practiced, they have moved themselves one step closer to the papacy! Every congregation of the body of Christ shall be judged faithful or unfaithful in these matters by Jesus; who is the head of the body!

Verse 7

"Purge out therefore the old leaven, that ye may be a new lump, as ye are unleavened. For even Christ our passover is sacrificed for us:"

The "old leaven" of this verse is analogous to the "old man" and the "works" associated with that life. The congregation and individuals as well, must rid themselves of that sin and its influence or "pay the price". Complete leavening or worse!

"…ye are unleavened"

Congregations and individuals who remain faithful (not perfect or sinless!) are represented as "unleavened dough" or cleansed, as they carry on the continuous "purging" process.

"**FOR** Christ , **OUR** Passover **IS** sacrificed for us."

I have bold typed three words in the quotation just used. Let's look at those words. "For", in the Greek, has been translated from the word "gar". Strong's #1063. Defined as: properly, assigning a reason. Therefore, Paul is going to tell them **why Corinth should be purging.**

The principal element in the genesis of the Passover, was the blood of the sacrificial lamb on the door lintel. Those exhibiting faith in that practice, (blood on the door lintel) escaped physical death on the night of those events. That event was memorialized once a year by the Jews (blood relatives of Jacob) for centuries. The keeping of that event was accomplished by first killing the lamb. From that point forward, their house must be purged of any and all leaven. If during the feast, any leaven was found, the whole house must be purged again. This festival, known as the feast of unleavened bread, and culminating in the Passover feast, lasted for a week. As long as the paschal lamb was in the house, the purging process continued.

Christians do not celebrate the paschal feast. (Even though there appears to have been some at Corinth who wanted to "borrow" some of those things for the N.T. Church. 1Cor 11) But the things of the O.T. were following the "patterns of the things in the heavens", (Heb 9:23) Because of those "patterns" (types), the pattern for the New Testament church will be an "overlay", or a fulfilling of those things. As one can see in a comparative study of the "old" and "new", the old was characterized in the physical. (ie literal kingdom etc) But the new is characterized by spiritual things. (i.e. "my kingdom is not of this world" - spiritual) Therefore the idea of "keeping the feast", as commanded in 1Cor. 5, may be practiced but **only** in the same way we observe "circumcision". Spiritually! (Circumcision of the heart i.e. a spiritual "cutting away") Therefore the "keeping of the feast" does **NOT** directly refer to the Lord's supper! Let's look farther.

Next Paul uses two words that **do** indicate our involvement in 'the feast" of 1Cor 5. "**OUR** passover **IS** slain".

Remember, "**for** (gar-explanation as to why we should purge our spiritual house) our passover **IS** slain." When their (the Jews) passover

53

(a literal lamb) was slain, their literal house was purged. If leaven was later found, that process started over. If then, as we make the spiritual (overlay) application, Paul says **OUR** (New Testament age) lamb **IS (present tense)** slain, in **our**[spiritual]house! Now! Will there ever be a time when it could be said that **OUR** passover is **NOT** slain? **NEVER!** He is once slain for all time! Therefore, will there ever be a time in the church or in a Christian's life when purging should **not** be going on? NO!! **NEVER!** Therefore, our whole lives are typified by the feast of unleavened bread! Which Paul says I **MUST** keep! And we should!

Verse 8

"Therefore, let **US** keep the feast, not with **old** leaven, neither with the leaven of malice and wickedness; but with the unleavened bread of sincerity and truth.

Without fail, the Greek word (Strong's # 1859) translated "the feast", refers to the feast of unleavened bread in part or whole. An interpretation that allows any other use of this word to reference the feast of unleavened bread, but in 1Cor. 5 is interpreted as the communion, is capricious and subjective! If the communion is in view, the writer of the Corinthian letter has "sincerity and truth" as elements to be broken in place of literal unleavened bread. In our many discussions with the "digressive" brethren, we rightfully contend that the literal unleavened bread is God's prescribed element that allows us to scripturally discern the body of Christ. Once the bread is made the body of Christ, we have no scripture to add another "layer" to the symbolism!

Furthermore, Paul in writing to the church at Colosse states, (Col 2:16) "Let no man therefore judge you in meat, or in drink, or in respect of an holyday, or of the new moon, or of the Sabbath days:

The term "holy day" is translated from the same word "the feast" in 1Cor 5:8 is translated from. In one place Paul is saying " Let us keep the feast", making us wrong not to observe what is being referenced. In the other, Paul is saying the giving of respect to "an holyday" is of no consequence. Both **must** be followed! **We need to respect the law of harmony in our interpretations!**

Since we are commanded to observe the Lord's supper, (New Testament) and not the feast of unleavened bread (Old Testament), Is there an interpretation that preserves the integrity of the spiritual

BAD ARGUMENT

tapestry? **Yes!!** The word of God must be used in a way that allows New Testament fulfillment of Old Testament shadows

Paul says for us to keep the feast, then forbids malice and wickedness be present. He commands sincerity and truth. Elements that have nothing to do with the elements commanded (fruit of the vine=blood and unleavened bread=body of Christ) when Paul specifically wrote to set the communion in order!!! 1Cor. 11:23ff

But if the feast commanded in 1cor 5:8 is "the true" of what the feast of unleavened bread is "the shadow," **ALL of the scriptures can be understood with clarity and harmony!** If purging of the physical house of the Israelites was commanded when the lamb had been slain, and that process continued until the sacrifice was consumed or removed, then our lives in the church are typical of the days of unleavened bread. As long as our sacrifice is slain, that purging process must continue unabated! Since the scriptures say Jesus is our sacrifice, being slain once for all time, when can the purging stop? **Not on this earth!**

WE, as Christians, do not religiously observe festivals as the Jews. We do not observe days as did the Jews. We do not observe the passover as did the Jews. The Jews were commanded to purge the physical house of literal leavening agents. We are commanded to purge our spiritual house of spiritual leavening agents, malice and wickedness. During the O.T. Feast of unleavened bread, they feasted on literal unleavened bread. We are commanded to keep the feast with the spiritual unleavened bread of sincerity and truth. For as long as our sacrifice can be said to be slain!

Therefore, the words, the grammar, the application, nor logic will support this text as a reference to the communion !

Does having communion with sinners in a congregation corrupt the whole congregation? Thereby making that congregation no longer the "body of Christ"!

A whole congregation is corrupted when the whole congregation becomes **participants** (i.e. "has fellowship") in corrupt worship. If the scriptural communion elements are or any element of corporate worship (worship when the whole church be come together) is practiced contrary to God's elements of worship, that body has lost those things that identify it for what it supposed to be. The body of Christ! That

55

body may be **A** church, ("called out") but it can not be identified as the **LORD"S** "called out"!

If having communion with sinners contaminates the whole, no one could have been salvaged from Sardis. If the use of false teachers makes true worship impossible, none of the churches of Galatia would have been considered the Lord's churches!

The discernment of the body and blood of Christ during communion requires **only** two things. Proper elements and **personal** examination! (1Cor. 11:2 & 11:28)

Verse 9

"I wrote unto you in an epistle not to company with fornicators:"

The context seems to shift slightly, although not moving away entirely from the handling of the problem with the fornicator. Apparently, Paul had written a previous letter to talk about fornicators but had not offered as much insight as he now offers.

There are contexts where the term "fornication" is very specific in its use. But as is the case in 1 Cor. 5, the word is used to name a "debauchee". In this case one who had morally illegal connections with his father's wife. When Paul reminded them of his previous prohibition, it was inclusive of all debauchery by anyone. But apparently, the church must have mistakenly understood that a brother was exempt from that command. Not so! *NO! Paul's point is that he was talking about Christians not pagans!*

"to company with"

To get a clear understanding of this term, one needs to look at its etymology. Since all New Testament scripture originated in koinine Greek,("on the street" Greek) our word study will always start there.

The phrase "to company with" in the Greek text is "sunanamignumi".

Strong's #4874 – defined as- to mix up".

Mr Strong also gives the etymology of the word. He states the origin of this word to be taken from Strong's #4862 **put together with #303 and #3396**

To entirely understand the original, let's look at the word "components" cited by Mr Strong .

#4862 – sun- defined as- a primary preposition denoting union with or together

(But much closer than #3326 & #3344)

#303 - - ana- defined as- properly, up

#3396- mignumi- defined as- primary verb-to mix

Therefore, we may understand "to company with" as used by the Spirit, to describe one who will " mix up together" with others. (in this text, fornicators)

Can the nature of this "mixing up together" be authoritatively defined to allow some things, while specifically excluding others? Let's check it out!

Under the definition of Strong's #4862, there is an addendum supplied (along with the scriptural text) that will help us better understand what kind of "mixing together with" is in view.

Mr Strong defines #4862 as "denoting union with or together". Then he cites two other Greek words. #3326 and 3844. He states that the union or togetherness that defines #4862 is closer than the union implied or defined by #3326 & #3344

#3326- meta- defined as – denoting accompaniment, "amid"

#3344- para- defined as – near, beside, vicinity, proximity, casual

Therefore, "to company with" (#4862) is **not** inclusive of merely being in a group or throng as #3326 would have indicated had the Spirit used that word.

Being physically "near, in proximity, or casual encounter" is **not** included in # 4862

Before drawing our final conclusion on the phrase, "to company with", it is imperative that we expose the text of the next two verses in this study.

Verse 10

"Yet not altogether with the fornicators of this world, or with the covetous, or an idolater, or extortioners, or with idolaters; for then ye must needs go out of this world."

Some Christians seem to overlook the language Paul uses in this verse. While many understand the prohibitions pronounced toward one called "a brother", some have no compunction in close alliances or associations with those guilty of these sins but not members of the

57

church. Paul does **not** sanction, or place divine approval on becoming "friends" ("close-fond") with the world in general. **Nor** one guilty of those sins listed in particular!

Yet Paul, does leave open enough association to accomplish the mission of the church; **to seek and save the lost!** Jesus was wrongly criticized for eating with publicans and sinners. But his intent is clearly revealed when He said' "The well need no physician, but the sick". With a great deal of clarity, one can understand the nature of his "keeping company" (eating , drinking, associating) with those people. He was not there to socialize, but save souls! Today there are still those whose want to play God in attaching motive to all "companying" that takes place. This is not always possible! Let us not judge one another in areas where infinite knowledge of motive is necessary.

The inspired writer also left enough leeway for Christians to be able to function in this world. Paul says if all contact with those guilty of these things were forbidden, one would have to leave this world! This kind of isolationism was clearly **not** the intent of the prohibition in Paul's charge, "not to keep company". Therefore Paul, assisted by the spirit, used words that would allow the contact that was needed, and no more!

** A Side Note

Some Christians seem to think isolation is the best tool we have in remaining free of the things of this world. As little contact as possible! This is not scriptural. The kingdom of Heaven is like leavening! It **MUST** mix to some degree to accomplish the work of the church on earth. I need to remember that!

Verse 11

"But now I have written unto you not to keep company, if any man that is called a brother be a fornicator, or covetous, or an idolater, or a railer, or a drunkard, or an extortioner; with such a one no not to eat."

Paul amplifies his earlier exhortation. "But now…" and "if any man that is call a brother" signifies our handling of brothers is somewhat different than an alien sinner. A brother who is "living in" such sins is not suitable to share a common meal with. That is my assertion. Now let's see if the words, grammar and context, are competent to support that statement!

We have studied somewhat extensively the term "to keep company". If the circumstances of this verse (sins enumerated) are present, the word "not" (#3361) negates or cancels the action. In other words, Christians are denied "mixing up together with" those who are guilty of the sins listed. The question remains. What does the phrase "no, not to eat." refer to. Common meal, or "the Lord's supper"?

"to eat"

Once again, let's look at the word definition and its corresponding etymology.

"to eat" - #4906 - sunesthio - Definition = to take food in company with
(from #4862 and #2068)

Like many other words, this Greek word "sunesthio", is a compound of two other words. Let's investigate the origin of "sunesthio".

#4862 - sun -Definition = a primary preposition denoting union with or together (but much closer than 3326 or 3344)

#2068 - esthio – Definition = to eat (usually literal)

Notice the correlation between #4874 (to keep company) and 4906 (to eat). Both activities involve a togetherness that transcends merely being in group with, or having proximity to an individual. Both indicate close social intercourse.

Paul first denies "mixing up together" socially, then defines eating a common meal (4906) as being within the parameters of that prohibition!

But the question may be asked. How can we be certain that this is not a reference to eating the Lord's supper?

First. In regards to the Lord's supper, (1 Cor. 11:28) we are to examine **ourselves**! 1Cor. 5:11 speaks of our "not companying" with those who **we** have examined and found guilty of specified sins.

Second. The silence of the scriptures forbids the use of "closed communion"! Insuring that those guilty of the sins specified do not partake of the "supper" would require an "inquisition" prior to each communion service.

BAD ARGUMENT

59

Third. The word "sunesthio" (def. – to take food in company with) is only used four times in the scriptures. Lets look at those passages.

Acts 10:41

41 Not to all the people, but unto witnesses chosen before of God, even to us, who **did eat** and drink with him after he rose from the dead.

The word "sunesthio" cannot possibly refer to the Lord's supper in this passage. Jesus told the "us" in Acts 10:41 that he would henceforth not eat "the supper" with them until he ate and drank it anew in his father's kingdom! (Matt 26:29) That same group was eating and drinking with him **after** he arose from the dead, but **before the establishment of the kingdom and the memorial service!**

Acts 11:3

3 Saying, Thou wentest in to men uncircumcised, and didst **eat** with them.

Once again, the "eating" is clearly with a group of people (uncircumcised – Gentiles) whose social intercourse Peter's Jewish brethren felt was still improper for Peter, being a Jew.

Galatians 2:12

12 For before that certain came from James, he did **eat** with the Gentiles: but when they were come, he withdrew and separated himself, fearing them which were of the circumcision.

Peter is yet again at the center of the controversy. Eating a common meal with Gentiles.

In none of the above references may we twist, bend, or misconstrue the intent of the words, or the context of the writer. The communion is **NOT** the intent of the inspired writer when he employs the word "sunesthio"!

Shall we then take the following passage and ascribe to it a meaning contrary to all other similar texts where the same word has been used? Not good hermeneutics!

1 Corinthians 5:11

11 But now I have written unto you **not to keep company**, if any man that is called a brother be a fornicator, or covetous, or an idolater,

or a railer, or a drunkard, or an extortioner; with such an one **no not to eat.**[11]

For one to thrust the communion into this passage in light of previous usage would be a clear case of eisegesis!

Fourth. Without fail, when the Lord's supper is in view, the Spirit always employs "phago" (# 5315 -to eat (lit. or fig.)), or "esthio". (#2068 – to eat (usually literal)). **NOT #4874!!**

Therefore, 1 Cor. 5:11 is not a competent text to support the application of "no not to eat" to the communion. To force that interpretation on the text is not only fallacious hermeneutics, but would also constitute intellectual dishonesty!

Verse 12 & 13

"For what have I to do to judge them also that are without? do not ye judge them that are within?

But them that are without God judgeth. Therefore put away from among yourselves that wicked person."

In the final two verses Paul clearly brings to view two groups of people. Those within, and those without. By context, and without contradiction from definitions or grammar, the intent is to address those "in Christ" and those "outside of Christ". In essence, Paul states; It is not our responsibility to pass sentence on those outside of Christ. (non members) We (the church) have no power or jurisdiction over them.

BUT...

If there is a hurtful, spiritual derelict among you, it is incumbent on you to recognize their choice and deny them open and close association. As has been defined by the terms **"not to keep company"** and **"no not to eat"**! They (the wicked person) have chosen to sever themselves from the fellowship of Jesus, therefore, they must also forfeit that which is an outgrowth of that partnership! Open Christian association!

Summary 1 Cor 5

The subject to be addressed is outlined by the Apostle in the opening sentence of this chapter. There was word "on the street" that Corinth had a serious morality problem and Paul confirms it! He further states, I'm not there in body, but this is what you need to do.

By the authority of Jesus, at a time when the whole church is together, his (the wicked person) choice of masters needs to be publicly made known. A difficult thing for the flesh but practiced in hope that the spirit may be salvaged.

He then explains the effect of leaven unexposed on the "whole lump". (congregation) Sin, like any agent of influence, must be identified and acted on. Else the whole is affected.

Paul then supplies the spiritual logic to the purging process. Since our passover, Jesus, **IS** slain, (purging starts when the lamb is slain and continues as long as the slain lamb is present) the purging process will be an ongoing endeavor. The "leavened bread" that is to be purged is malice and wickedness. The residue after purging (or "the unleavened bread") is " the new lump" of "sincerity and truth".

Paul then moves on to clarify an apparent earlier letter concerning who "to company with" and who "not to company with". He makes a clear distinction between "a wicked brother" and an alien sinner.

Finally in verse 11, he concludes the matter on cleansing the church. He tells them (the church) not to "mix up together" with a "wicked" brother. Then makes that inclusive of "with such a one no not to eat". (indicative of a common meal)

Addendum to 1Cor. 5 exposition
2 Cor 7:11-12

11 For behold this selfsame thing, that ye sorrowed after a godly sort, what carefulness it wrought in you, yea, what clearing of yourselves, yea, what indignation, yea, what fear, yea, what vehement desire, yea, what zeal, yea, what revenge! <u>IN ALL THINGS YE HAVE APPROVED YOURSELVES TO BE CLEAR IN THIS MATTER.</u>

This writer believes the last phrase indicates culpability of at least leadership, and probably others as well, had they not acted in good faith on Paul's advice. May we, as faithful servants in God's house, be diligent and not slothful in our attempts to understand and follow His word in regard to cleansing of the body! Every Christian in the body has **some** responsibility to act.

****

In the beginning of this writing endeavor, several texts were introduced that by use or abuse play a prominent role in any discussion on true worship and fellowship. I will continue to address these passages.

1 John 1:1-7

1:1 **That** which was from the beginning, which we **have heard**, which we **have seen** with our eyes, which we **have looked upon**, and our **hands have handled**, of the Word of life;

2 (For **the life** was manifested, and we **have seen it**, and **bear witness**, and **shew** unto you **that eternal life**, which was with the Father, and was manifested unto us;)

3 **That** which **we have seen** and heard declare we unto you**, that ye also may have fellowship with us:** and truly our fellowship is with the Father, and with his Son Jesus Christ.

4 And these things write we unto you, that your joy may be full.

5 **This** then is the message which we have heard of him, and declare unto you, that God is light, and in him is no darkness at all.

6 If we say that we have fellowship with him, and walk in darkness, we lie, and do not the truth:

7 But if we walk in the light, as he is in the light, we have fellowship one with another, and the blood of Jesus Christ his Son cleanseth us from all sin.

Trying to understand fellowship without an exposition of this text would be pointless. It has been used and abused by the pugnacious, the sectarian, the Pharisaical, the honestly ignorant and the misled! Nearly every "splinter" faction of the church of Christ has laid claim to this scripture! In belief (or hope) that it would support their latest foray into what they **deny** is the division of the body of Christ. But when practiced according to traditional interpretation, does just that! Divides brethren! Yet in each successive division, both parties claim **they** are the "true" church of Christ! Walking "in the light as He is in the light".

It may come as a surprise to some, but 1 John 1:7 will **not** support **any** division of the body of Christ!

Let's look at the text.

Usually, (as is the case with most misapplications) 1John 1:7 is quoted as a "stand alone" text. When we so use the scriptures, our "proof text" becomes a pretext on which a false premise is built. Context **must** be considered to extract the writer's intent!

1 John 1:7

But if we walk in the light, as he is in the light, we have fellowship one with another, and the blood of Jesus Christ his Son cleanseth us from all sin.

As I have done in other texts, let's talk about what this verse does **NOT** say first. Light cannot be equated with truth, even though "light" **does** encompass truth. If that were the case, one would have to possess or walk in **all** truth so that we could "have fellowship" with one another. This verse makes fellowship with each other conditional on our walking "in the light **AS** he is in the light".

Thayer defines "as" as:

NT:5613   hoos

as, like as, even as, according as, in the same manner as,

Therefore, **if** light represents truth, and our fellowship is based on **all** that truth, we must possess or walk **in** that infinite truth, else our fellowship with one another is non-existant! That interpretation makes fellowship impossible by demanding our walk in "light" (all truth?) is "in the same manner as" Jesus Christ.

Some would assert "in the light" indicates direction. Yet when looking at the original, "in" is translated from **en** in the Greek.

NT:1722 en (en); a primary preposition denoting (fixed) position (in place, time or   state), and (by implication) instrumentality (medially or constructively)

Had the spirit intended to convey direction rather than (fixed) position, there is no dearth of vocabulary with the Spirit! Toward (Strong's 4314) is a word that conveys direction! It was **not** employed! Therefore, whatever one interprets "in the light " to be, that interpretation must embody a position held, and not merely a direction pursued! **That interpretation will bury us in subjectivism!** If one uses that interpretation, one could make no universal application of the text, since my idea regarding the direction or progress of an individual or congregation might be substantially different than yours! An appeal for truth must rest in the scriptures and not in man to make those judgments.

What is the LIGHT of 1 John 1:7?

Let's look at the whole text of 1John 1 again.

1 John 1

1:1 THAT which was from the beginning, which we have HEARD, which we have SEEN with our eyes, which we have looked upon, and our hands have HANDLED, of the Word of life;

The word, "that"is a demonstrative pronoun specifying something in particular. Therefore our interpretation of this verse and the following body of scripture **must** embrace and identify who or what **"that"** is specified to be!

Then John begins to specify with five descriptive phrases what **"that"** is.

THAT:

1. was <u>from the beginning</u> (eternal existence)
2. [that] we (the apostles etal) <u>have heard</u>
3. we <u>have seen</u> (physically discern)
4. we <u>have looked upon</u> (contemplated or studied intently)
5. our <u>hands have handled</u> (verified by touch and manipulation)

This verse is concluded with **"of the Word of life"**.

The word "of" is translated from the Greek word "peri" which means "concerning or about". Therefore, in essence, John is saying we are here to verify "the [eternal] life" embodied in Jesus Christ! Therefore, the **"that"** of verse one is specifically eternal life embodied in Jesus. Eternal life cannot be a reality outside of the rock-solid truth that Jesus **is** the Son of God!!

2 (For the life was manifested, and we have seen it, and bear witness, and shew unto you that eternal life, which was with the Father, and was manifested unto us;)

John further testifies concerning the veracity of his previous claims. Twice concerning "the life" (eternal), the word "manifested" is used. I believe the closeness of definitions of "manifested" and "light" to be no accident. For "manifested" means "to render apparent". The original root of the word "manifest" will allow a relationship to the word "light" which means "to shine". It would not be in error to render the passage: (For the life [eternal] became apparent, and we have seen it, we are eyewitnesses and that eternal life that was with the Father was made apparent unto us.

3 That which we have seen and heard declare we unto you, that ye also may have fellowship with us: and truly our fellowship is with the Father, and with his Son Jesus Christ.

"That which" cannot be attributed any identification without context being examined. The grammar and words used in verse 1 & 2 have clearly identified the object of John's declaration. The [eternal] Life! In Christ!

In this verse there is no subject change. The "that which" of verse 3 is synonymous with the same phrase in verse 1.

"and truly". In a manifest, unconcealed fashion. " our fellowship", our participation and/or partnership is with the father and the son.

Verse three may be rendered thus: The Eternal life that we (apostles) have looked at, touched, and examined, we are announcing to you. So that you (we/us, all Christians) may be participants and partners with us (apostles): and truly, (manifestly, without concealment) our participation/partnership is with the Father and his Son, Jesus Christ.

4 And these things write we unto you, that your joy may be full.

We (the apostles) write these things (those aforementioned) so that you (we/us, all Christians) may be "crammed full" of cheerfulness.

5 This then is the message which we have heard of him, and declare unto you, that God is light, and in him is no darkness at all.

Therefore, this (what John was about to announce) is the announcement Jesus told us to announce to you. (us/all Christians) God is illumination, (that which makes manifest or apparent) and in Jesus is no obscurity. (shadiness, shadows)

6 If we say that we have fellowship with him, and walk in darkness, we lie, and do not the truth:

If we (us/all Christians) claim to have partnership with (as co-participants in the "life") God (Jesus) and tread about (walk/live our lives) in the shadows and obscurity (as if we are unenlightened about who Jesus is) we (us) do not tell the truth. (We are not living our profession.) We are NOT partners with God.

7   But if we walk in the light, as he is in the light, we have fellowship one with another, and the blood of Jesus Christ his Son cleanseth us from all sin.

****

If there is a chance of our understanding the subject of fellowship, we must strive for a correct interpretation of 1 John 1:7. Or at least not allow the scripture to be used in a twisted or patently incorrect way. To be able to arrive at a correct exegesis, let's first deal with some objectionable interpretations.

****

1Jn. 1:7 is another scripture that has been "claimed" and used by nearly every sect or party whose roots appear to pass through the "Stone/ Cambell movement". It is not the intent, right, nor the inclination of this writer to cast aspersions or to judge those men or anyone else. But the "true light" revealed by their study (as is the case with all studies) shall be put to the test of intense scrutiny by those of us who live after them. However, since they were just human, their words, interpretations and conclusions must not be allowed to become the orthodoxy or creed or guiding principles of the body of Christ! Let God's word "be true and every man a liar"!

The generation immediately preceding this writer had its men "who were chief" among us. Their words, messages, sermons shall be "tried" in the same fashion all religious things must be tested. By the Bible! Yet by adopting the "restoration slogan", "we speak where the Bible speaks and are silent where the Bible is silent", the "we" of 1Jn 1:7, has been made synonomous with every schismatic spawned by "wrested scriptures"!

The men of preceding generations who made interpretations of certain texts, appear to be able to speak with the authority of those who have their names enshrined in the foundation of the Holy City! For today, when one makes an independent study and arrives at a conclusion different from the "restoration fathers" or preeminent preachers, one may be branded "heretical", "radical", or simply "isolated" from "the faithful". In essence 1John 1:7 is "ripped" from its contextual, and definitive underpinning, and is used by individuals and groups to justify their exclusive hold on being **THE** true and **The** "faithful" church.

Most preachers in the church of Christ believe "in the light" to describe the doctrines they hold to be true at a particular time. To "walk in darkness" is defined (by their application) as one who "walks" contrary to doctrine that "chief brothers" have elevated as "important", "big", or of major consequence. One may be ignorant or contrary on multiple subjects, but not the "big" ones! The interpretation of walking "in the light" will change depending on which factional element one enquires of! Thereby making the so-called "test of fellowship" not a Biblical "test" at all! But rather, a regional, congregational, factional, or even a subjective judgment call. Brethren, the inspired words will not yield to this interpretive method! If we continue down this interpretive path, that "glorious church" shall continue to appear invalid and inadequate to accomplish all we have been commissioned to do! **SAVE THE LOST!!**

Whatever "in the light" entails, that interpretation and application must be universally true! That "walk" must identify and epitomize ALL who have fellowship with that one whose blood cleanses us from all iniquity. The most common schismatic version of 1Jn. 1:7 should read thus: "If you walk in the knowledge and understanding I have today and what we believe important, we will have fellowship with you". Fifty years ago, you (or your parents) were where "they" are to day. For those who died in that era, does that mean because of their ignorance, (or our growth, etc.) that you hold no hope for their eternal estate? Or would you hold hope for those, but those who may be at that point of understanding (or ignorance) today, "have not God"? These questions are not posed to confuse, but are that which can help us to lower the number of possible interpretations.

Then there is the interpretation which embraces the necessity of growth, but still would interpret "walking in the light" to be indicative of "direction". Or in other terms, it's the "they're coming our way" interpretation. Almost any problem may remain indefinitely at a congregation if an influential preacher or brother "sees improvement"! Subjective to the core!!

But notice the word "in". In the Greek, that word is translated from "en". Mr Strong defines that (#1722) as the preposition of position. As has been previously stated, had the Spirit wanted to indicate "direction", the Greek word "pros" (#4314) was available. "Pros" is defined as the preposition of direction. Therefore, for one to impose an interpretation on 1Jn. 1:7 that the words used by the Spirit are not competent to support, will only impugn the omnipotent vocabulary of God! Therefore, the "they're coming our way" (improving) interpretation appears rooted in personal observation.

Let's examine this interpretation deeper.

If "they're coming our way" is to be used as criteria for determining who is walking "in the light", **who** shall judge? **AND** what scriptural guidelines shall be cited so that **ALL** may universally know and apply those rules? In the past, personal judgments have been made. But those conclusions have not been shared by all who observed. Therefore, the "they're coming our way" interpretation of walking "in the light" is once again proved subjective and **must** be incorrect!

And, furthermore.....

If one is of the persuasion that walking "in the light" encompasses truth "**as** he is in the light", will that interpretation not demand that our fellowship with one another be relegated on our understanding **ALL** the truth? For, the Greek word "hoos", (Strongs #5613) is defined by Mr Thayer as "in the same fashion as". Therefore, by making "light" equate to truth, our fellowship with one another could only be realized by our knowing and holding **all** the truth! (i.e. a brotherhood consensus) "In the same fashion" Jesus knows and holds **ALL** the truth! If one's interpretation of a text makes human obedience to that text impossible, that interpretation is incorrect! The equation of "the light" in 1 John 1:7 with the whole body of scriptural truth, will render "horizontal" fellowship impossible! Therefore, light in 1Jn 1:7 is **not** synonymous with **ALL** truth!

This has been a long segment, but necessary nonetheless. Misconceptions (spiritual rubbish) need to be cleared away before "choice vine" can be planted.

What meaning should be attributed to 1 John 1:7?
The following is a more "in depth" look at **THE LIGHT.**

Let's begin with Luke 2:25-32.

25 And, behold, there was a man in Jerusalem, whose name was Simeon; and the same man was just and devout, waiting for the **consolation** of Israel: and the Holy Ghost was upon him.

26 And it was revealed unto him by the Holy Ghost, that he should not see death, before he had seen the Lord's **Christ**.

27 And he came by the Spirit into the temple: and when the parents brought in the child **Jesus**, to do for him after the custom of the law,

28 Then took he him up in his arms, and blessed God, and said,

29 Lord, now lettest thou thy servant depart in peace, according to thy word:

30 For mine eyes have seen thy **salvation**,

31 Which thou hast prepared before the face of all people;

32 A **light** to lighten the Gentiles, and the glory of thy people Israel.

What Simeon saw: CONSOLATION-HOPE
                    THE CHRIST
                    JESUS
                    SALVATION
                    LIGHT

Light ......def.---illumination or that which makes manifest

DARKNESS....def.----- shadiness or obscurity

LIGHT-------   Allows understanding—therefore change—dispels fear of unknown

DARKNESS -----will obscure understanding and breeds fear

Nothing man contemplates is quite as foreboding AS the question:

IF A MAN DIE, SHALL HE LIVE AGAIN?

John 11:25-28 Jesus and Martha at the death of her brother, Lazarus

25 Jesus said unto her, I am the **resurrection**, and **the life**: he that believeth in me, though he were dead, yet shall he live:

26 And whosoever liveth and believeth in me shall never die. Believest thou this?

27 She saith unto him, Yea, Lord: I believe that thou art the Christ, the Son of God, which should come into the world.

Was he **literally** "the resurrection"... or.....the **proof** of it?
Was he **literally** "the life"................or.... the **proof** of it?

70

John 1:4 The question is answered with great clarity!

4 In him was [eternal] **life**; and <u>the [eternal]</u> **life** was <u>the</u> **light** of men. **Literally a light or illumination of a fact. Within Him was power of eternal life!!**

John 9:5

5 As long as I am in the world, I am <u>the</u> **light** of the world.
The work of the father, which he came to do, would be finished when he left the earth.

QUESTION:
What happened to **the light** when He left the world? **Flash in the pan? The world left with no light?**

Let's let the scriptures speak!

2 Cor 4:3-8

3 But if our **gospel** be hid, it is hid to them that are lost:
4 In whom the god of this world hath blinded the minds of them which believe not (*they were living in darkness and obscurity*), lest **the light** of the glorious **gospel** <u>of Christ</u>, (*concerning Christ*) who is the image of God, should shine unto them.
5 For we preach not ourselves, but Christ Jesus the Lord; and ourselves your servants for Jesus' sake.
6 For God, who commanded the light to shine out of darkness, hath shined in our hearts, to give **the light** of (*concerning*) the knowledge of the glory of God in the face (*VIEW-reality*) of Jesus Christ.
7 But we have this treasure (***WHAT TREASURE?***) (<u>*knowledge of God through JC*</u>) in earthen vessels, that the excellency of the power may be of God, and not of us.
Against that backdrop, let's move back to 1Jn 1

1 John 1:1-3
1:1 That which was from the beginning, which we have heard, which we have seen with our eyes, which **we have looked upon**, and

our hands have handled, of [*concerning or with respect to*] the Word of life;

2(For **the life** was manifested, and we have seen it, and bear WITNESS, and shew unto you that **ETERNAL LIFE**, which was with the Father, and was **MANIFESTED** unto us;)

3 **THAT** which we have **SEEN AND HEARD** declare we unto you, that (*or so that*) ye also may **HAVE FELLOWSHIP** with us: and truly **OUR FELLOWSHIP** is with the Father, and with his Son Jesus Christ.

The following is redundant, but necessary to the exposition.

FELLOWSHIP----- Def.—partnership / share in a thing
GRAMMATICALLY---KJV---**NOUN EVERYTIME!!**

Not something you do but something you have!!!

Therefore John is giving information so that we might be able to have a share in the same things he, and the rest of the apostles had a share in! I.E. That eternal life in Christ, THE light of the world!!!

1 John 1:4-8
4 And **these things** write we unto you, that your joy may be full.

5 This then is the message which we have heard of him, and declare unto you, that God is light, and in him is no darkness at all.

6 If we say that we have fellowship (***PARTNERSHIP or SHARE***) with him, and walk in darkness, (*do not know him nor can one in darkness have a share in eternal life*) we lie, and do not the truth:

7 But if we walk in the light, as he is in the light, we have fellowship one with another, and the blood of Jesus Christ his Son cleanseth us from all sin.

Therefore, wherever we contact the blood "that cleanseth us from all sin", THERE is the "light" of 1John 1:7! We are "in Christ" and he is in us. We rise (from baptism) to walk a new eternal life in Christ!

Look at the conversions in the book of Acts.

Day of Pentecost

Paul -- Household of Cornelius

Philippian jailer--- Samaritans by Phillup--- etc.

Paul recounts his conversion to king Agrippa

Acts 26:16-20

16 But rise, and stand upon thy feet: for I have appeared unto thee for this purpose, to make thee a minister and a witness both of these things which thou hast seen, and of those things in the which I will appear unto thee;

17 Delivering thee from the people, and from the Gentiles, unto whom now I send thee,

18 To open their eyes, and to turn them from **darkness to light**, and from the power of Satan unto God, [so] that they may receive **forgiveness of sins**, and **inheritance** among them which are sanctified by faith that is in me.

19 Whereupon, O king Agrippa, I was not disobedient unto the heavenly vision:

ANNANIAS- Arise and be baptized and wash away thy sins!!

***Notice the connection between "darkness to light" and the reception of "forgiveness of sins, and inheritance."**

John 1:4

4 In him was life; and the life *was the light* of men

When Paul or anyone is obedient to the heavenly vision, they move from darkness to light.

They move from "sin and death" to forgiveness and life.

They move from the shadow of death to light and "life eternal"!!

They move from being "a nobody", into the family of God and therefore an heir!!

1 Peter 2:9-11

9 But ye are a chosen generation, a royal priesthood, an holy nation, a peculiar people; that ye should shew forth the praises of him who hath **called** you **out of darkness into** his marvelous **light:**

10 Which in time past were **not a people**, but **are now** the people of God: which had **not obtained mercy**, but **NOW**, have obtained mercy.

JOHN said we become "his people". (partners/fellows) Therefore, partners and participants with God, in the LIGHT—THE GOSPEL!! That which extols "life" to all who obey him!!!

THEREFORE

When I understand someone has fellowship with God as did Paul, or as I, we then recognize one another as partners (HAVE FELLOWSHIP) in the same thing (the gospel - the life eternal) together with God!!! We become "yokefellows" and "fellowlaborers" in Christ. **We have fellowship one with another! 1 John 1:7**

Gal 2:9 The "extention of fellowship"

9 And when James, Cephas, and John, who seemed to be pillars, **perceived** the grace that was given unto me, they gave to me and Barnabas the right hands of fellowship; that we should go unto the heathen, and they unto the circumcision.

Fellowship was not "extended" or offered. The "right hand" was extended as signification or recognition of fellowship that already existed. Much as we would recognize co-operation today.

Gal 2:9 illustrates, with clarity, the preceding point of 1John 1:7.

NOTE: Gal. 2:9 will be more fully discussed in a later chapter

---

Brothers and sisters!! Do not force an interpretation on 1 JN 1:7 or Gal 2:9 that will lead to a fracturing and splintering of the body! This will make the understanding and universal application of the BIBLE A VIRTUAL IMPOSSIBILITY!!!

Lets look at another of the "abused and misused" texts.
1JOHN 4:6
*1 Beloved believe not every spirit, but try the spirits whether they are of God: because m*any false prophets are gone out into the world.

2 Hereby know ye the Spirit of God: Every spirit that confesseth that Jesus Christ is come in the flesh is of God:

3 And every spirit that confesseth not that Jesus Christ is come in the flesh is not of God: and this is that spirit of antichrist, whereof ye have heard that it should come; and even now already is it in the world.

4 Ye are of God, little children, and have overcome them: because greater is he that is in you, than he that is in the world.

5 They are of the world: therefore speak they of the world, and the world heareth them.

6 We are of God: he that knoweth God heareth us; he that is not of God heareth not us. Hereby know we the spirit of truth, and the spirit of error.

The misuse of this passage centers around the misinterpretation of vs. 6. This is another passage that has been "uprooted" from its contextual "soil" and misused by factions in the body of Christ. Even in the controversy on fellowship, this scripture is used to support partisan interpretations!

Brothers, let's get one thing clear at the outset! None of "us" are the "us" of 1 Jn. 1:6!!

Those who are of God hear the **apostles**! They (the apostles) were eyewitnesses (the ONLY reliable witnesses) to the incarnation of the Christ. There were those in John's day, as ours, who would not confess (believe) that Jesus is come in the flesh. (ie. Gnostics) John says, "If they (of this world) will not hear our (the eyewitnesses) testimony, they (who will not hear) are not of God.

If one considers the context of 1John 4:6, the "spirit of truth" may not be defined by a factional group as "the truth" being revealed by those who agree with that party on an "elevated" doctrine. (i.e. convenience worship, gold, no-gold, D&R, etc,) If the Bible is to be interpreted in that fashion, we shall never "untangle" the book!! And furthermore, we shall not be able to work with one another long enough to even try to attain unity in the bond of peace.

Therefore, those that hear the testimony of the eyewitnesses (the apostles) are "of God". Those not "of God" (the world) listen to the "misleading spirit". (spirit of error)

Do not mistake and equate a man's interpretation for inspiration!!
Yes! That includes mine as well! **The scriptures are inspired. Let the
inspired words say <u>all</u> they say, and no more!!!!**

Gal 1:6-9

In our discussion of fellowship, Gal 1:8 must be considered.
This verse is another used to support ongoing "partisanship" within
the kingdom. The "some" of verse 7 has been interpreted to be any
teacher or preacher who dared step outside the doctrinal status quo of
"brotherhood orthodoxy"! Or any brother who would dare question the
"mantra" of the "brotherhood paper". Or perhaps any brother whose
words "threaten" the " brotherhood power structure" no one wants
to admit exists! **"The gospel"** of Gal. 1:8 has been misconstrued to
encompass as many scriptural truths as **"the light** of 1John 1:7!

The question is: does Gal. 1:8 teach that concept? Like the discussion
on other scriptures in this study, one cannot "explain the words away"!
I will not try! The authority of scripture must stand. Neither should we
make this study a self-serving eisegesis. That has been the case with this
scripture and others as well!

Gal 6:6-9

**6 I marvel that ye are so soon removed from him that called you
into the grace of Christ unto another gospel:**

**7 Which is not another; but there be some that trouble you, and
would pervert the gospel of Christ.**

**8 But though we, or an angel from heaven, preach any other
gospel unto you than that which we have preached unto you, let
him be accursed.**

**9 As we said before, so say I now again, If any man preach
any other gospel unto you than that ye have received, let him be
accursed.**

Paul's concern and warning to the Galatian brethren is unmistakable
and one should not scoff at situations to which this verse applies. But
make no mistake, the inerrant words of the spirit shall give us "light"
(illumination-to know) on "the gospel" of vs. 7.

76

There are primarily two words used in the New Testament from which "gospel" is translated.

Verse 7-----Strongs #2098.... Def. --- good news [not the announcement of good news, but **the good news**]

euaggelion

Since this cannot be used as the good news announced **by** Christ, then it **MUST** be the good news **CONCERNING** Christ!

Verse 8-----Strongs 2097.... Def .---- the announcement of good news.

euaggelizo

So then, Paul is telling the Galatian brethren, if any one announces "good news" contrary to that which the apostles had announced, it is a perversion of the true and not "good news" at all!! The "perverted gospel" is a twisted or mutated version. That, [twisted version] and the herald of it is to be rejected!!

One begs to question! What, specifically, is **THE GOSPEL**, or "good news"?

Paul gives us an indication, at least, in the introduction of this thought in verse 6. He claims astonishment at how quickly they removed themselves from the "grace of God" **UNTO** another gospel. Therefore if they had left the "grace of God" for "another Gospel", Paul's announcement, [of good news] whom they first obeyed put them **IN** "the grace of God"! Since grace (getting what we don't deserve) is a spiritual blessing, and "**ALL** spiritual blessings" are in Christ, (Eph. 1: 2-3) **THE** Gospel is that which explains my opportunity to receive **ALL** those blessings!!

Now notice Paul's more specific declaration of **the gospel.**

1 Cor 15:1-7

1 Moreover, brethren, I declare unto you **the gospel** which I preached unto you, which also ye have received, and **wherein ye stand**;

2 **By which also ye are saved**, if ye keep in memory what I preached unto you, unless ye have believed in vain.

3 For **I delivered** unto you first of all that which I also received, **how that Christ died for our sins** according to the scriptures;

4 And that he was **buried,** and that he **rose** again the third day according to the scriptures:

5 **And that he was seen** of Cephas, then of the twelve:

6 After that, **he was seen** of above five hundred brethren at once; of whom the greater part remain unto this present, but some are fallen asleep.

7 After that, **he was seen** of James; then of all the apostles.

The **gospel** is the reality of our savior's death, burial and resurrection!!

THEREFORE, since HE lives, SO CAN WE!!!!!

That's THE GOSPEL, or the biggest hoax ever perpetrated on the human race!!!!!!!

THAT'S THE GOSPEL !

Paul declared "the gospel" unto the church at Corinth and said "wherein ye stand". Evidently, **"The gospel"** did **not** include the practicing, or knowledge of the whole body of revealed truth, since that church had several doctrinal errors, morality problems, and had not properly purged the body! Corinth still "stood" in the gospel in spite of doctrinal and morality problems! So may the same be said of a church today! To say that a congregation of the body of Christ "stands in the Gospel" is not tacit approval of **all** that may be present at that congregation. Sardis stood in the Gospel, but only a few were approved by Jesus.

The Contribution and fellowship

Any discussion on fellowship must look at the contribution made by all Christians and its relationship to fellowship and worship. For the question may legitimately be asked: "How can I give as I'm prospered at a congregation where those funds may be used to support people ("false" teachers) or things I don't agree with?" This **is** a legitimate question and needs to be addressed.

What is the relationship between contribution, distribution, and fellowship? Strong's #2842 is once translated contribution in Rom. 15:26. And once translated distribution in 2 Cor. 9:13. Those who translated from the Greek clearly understood that the "koinonia" of Rom. 15:26 and 2 Cor. 9:13 could not be translated as 1Jn. 1:7 and still convey the intent of the writer. To define Strong's #2842

78

as "partnership" or "participation" each time #2842 is used, will not allow the two scriptures cited to completely fit their context. But if we understand "contribution" and "distribution" to involve "a benefaction", or gift, those terms certainly remain firmly connected to partnership or participation. Those who are participants (have fellowship) with Jesus were participants in a benefaction for others who have fellowship [in the gospel] with Jesus.

Are all equally responsible for the distribution of the contribution?

Or. More specifically, if one contributes funds, but the distribution of those funds are deemed unscriptural, will God hold the contributor responsible? Does improper use of funds make all who attend and contribute false worshippers? Does the improper use of funds make all who "give" a "partaker of evil deeds"? Or is one guilty if only **certain** doctrines (exception, conv. worship, etc) are present?

I believe there are two or three areas of scripture that needs our observation. First, let's look at paying taxes. From the time of Jesus, there has always been the question: "Since I believe the government uses my money for unscriptural things, (war, abortion, feeding those who won't work, etc) must I pay taxes?" Jesus, in Matt 22:21, plainly answers that question. Also commanding Peter in Matt 17:27 to pay the "tribute". By so doing, does that make Peter and the Lord participants or partners (i.e. having fellowship) in the excesses and atrocities of Rome?!! Does **YOU** paying taxes indicate participation (fellowship) in the wickedness of the U.S. government? i.e. abortion, war,etc.

If a woman (or a man) contributes faithfully to the Lord, but the congregation where she worships calls a teacher she believes wrong or detrimental, may **she/he** still be able to truly worship? If she continues to contribute, does she have fellowship in all that is wrongly supported? If so, God is placing responsibility where he gives no power of control. Can't be true!

Does God consider a woman to "have fellowship" (she **is** a partner) with **ALL** that her husband does, right or wrong? No way!

All of the above illustrations prove, beyond reasonable doubt, a Bible principle. **God holds one responsible, proportionate to the authority or power to act!!**

Therefore in regard to the contribution, **each** has been given the command and the power to "give as you have prospered". Each Christian has the power to act on that command. However, in matters of distribution, the same will not be true. Those who have made the **contribution** have not been empowered by God to oversee the **distribution**. Since women, and the men **not** in a leadership role, have no authority in distribution, they, by the reasoning of some, have only two choices. If they disagree on distribution or preacher decisions, etc., stop giving, or leave the congregation. That would make them disobedient to the precept of giving and worshipping in spirit and in truth. Scripturally, God shall hold responsible all those he has commanded and empowered to contribute, (that would be each one who has prospered) and additionally responsible, all those he has empowered (that would be the leadership) to oversee the distribution!

This is not a new concept. Yet sometimes, when congregations are being designated as "unfaithful" by men, the contribution is used as an excuse not to worship where "true worship" **could** take place. This objection is used only in "certain" situations. Consensus is rare (nor required) in most church decisions. This objection is raised by men who **know** that agreement on distribution does not **always** occur! And never has!!! Fellowship, nor the worship has been affected! Therefore, when men make decisions that I may not agree with, but which do **not** necessitate my participation, God will not hold me responsible! **See Sardis!!** He will hold me responsible for that which I can do. Give!

Communion

Since the word "koinonia" is translated both fellowship and communion (along with contribution and distribution), the relationship of these two words needs to be handled. For men have long put forth the idea that having communion involves all (by joint participation) who "commune". Therefore, (the reasoning goes) if one (or the whole congregation) "communes" with an unrepentant reveler, all who "commune" have a part in that sin. If the congregational leadership is in error as to what constitutes that sin, therefore does not act accordingly, the worship of that entire congregation is vain or false or both! That's the position taken by some. Even though Sardis, and the other churches of Asia **do not** prove that true!

Again, one of the reasons people have been deceived and misled on fellowship is the misuse and entanglement of words and their definitions. In this segment of study, the abuse of texts involves the words fellowship, communion and commune. We, (including me in the past) have always supposed that "communing" involves everybody in everything. When in actuality, "communing" or "commune" is **not** a New Testament word. Our misconception occurred when we did the same to the term communion as we have done with fellowship. We changed a noun to a verb.

Now brethren, this is not just a matter of semantics. I understand the changes in language and that words over time come to signify different things. If a church member speaks of "communing", I know the communion is in view. But when we are trying to **understand** what Paul meant when **he** spoke of "the **communion** of the blood of Christ", we must respect the authority of the words used by Paul. We must respect the grammar employed by the Spirit to convey **His** message.

The word "commune" is a verb. It is **NEVER** used in the New Testament even remotely connected with communion. It is used 4 times in the past tense, but unfailingly refers to communication! (speaking with another) Therefore when we refer to "having communion" as "communing" we change what the spirit intended as an object to be participated in (body and blood of Christ) into action one engages in. The meaning foisted on communion then involves the whole congregation as participating in all the sins (sinners) present in that assembly! That's preposterous!! We are all "priests" (see 1Pet. 2:5&9) participating **in** the sacrifice (the body of the Christ) for our sins.

1 Cor 10:15-18

15 I **speak as to wise men**; judge ye what I say.

16 The **cup of blessing** which we bless, is **it** not the **communion** of the blood of Christ? The **bread** which we break, is **it** not the **communion** of the body of Christ?

17 For we being many are one bread, and one body: **for we are all partakers of that one bread.**

18 Behold Israel after the flesh: are not they which eat of the sacrifices partakers of the alter

This text points out in a clear fashion that the participation that defines communion is participation **in** the body (bread- the sacrifice) and the blood (fruit of the vine) and **not** participation **IN** one another! The connection all in the congregation have to one another is in the benefit of the sacrifice. Having communion with Christ does not breed spiritual disease!! Sin cannot be passed by use of the common container or in communion in general. Thank God!

Today, when we go from the Biblical, "having fellowship" to "disfellowship", we distort the language of the spirit and abuse the texts. We make the fellowship of Jesus something we extend and something we take away. We make fellowship something we do and not something we have. By the same token, when we interchange "having communion" with "communing", we have tampered with divine language. Communion is the participation we have in the sacrifice for our sins. Communing is what we do when we talk with some one. Brothers, this is not a case of quibbling, or merely semantics, but allowing God to say what he intends! And no more!! **Therefore, having communion with Jesus in the presence of sinners does not of necessity make me a sinner!!** So indicates the church at Sardis! Etal!

What about false teachers?

There has probably never been a discussion about fellowship that did not include false teachers. How should we handle those who teach or believe different than me? What is their effect on a congregation? **Exactly** who **are** the false teachers of the Bible? To whom shall this dreaded label be attached? Is everyone who differs with you or me a false teacher? Is there a person who is a "sincerely mistaken" teacher? Or is he only considered "sincere" if he doesn't disagree with me on my "big" issues? Or perhaps if he has not run amuck with some of those "who seem to be somewhat" among us? How can we tell the difference? Or shall this stigma only be attached for **certain** errors? And which ones? Whose, or even better, **WHAT** list shall we use so that universal application may occur? Can anyone be saved who worships at a congregation where "false teachers" (on any subject) seem to be in charge?

I could probably go on with questions on this subject. But the aforementioned shall suffice to encourage your own legitimate questions. I wish I could claim "neat, tidy" answers to all these questions. But for this writer, there still remains some obscurity in some areas of this study. Where clarity of issue is not possible, I shall respect those in charge at each congregation.

Some may feel the lack of sufficient clarity in this segment casts suspicion on this treatise as a whole. However, that logic (part wrong- all wrong) would preclude our understanding the Bible. As is the case in all areas of this study, enlightenment is sought and welcomed! The fruit of your scholarly efforts are thankworthy. Please share with this writer those fruits.

Although I understanding the degree of difficulty in this subtopic, I believe there to be enough clarity in scripture to allow **some** answers. The relationship of false teachers to the subjects of true worship and fellowship needs to be better understood.

In regards to false teachers, the following text (and others) has been appropriated and made to apply to almost every person who dared speak contrary to a faction's "elevated" doctrine. Not **every** doctrine, just the ones elevated to "important" by those influential among us. Does it truly apply; or has there been an "embezzlement" of text?

Let's check it out!

2 Peter 2

1 But there were **false prophets** also among the people, **even as** there shall be **false teachers** among you, who **privily** shall bring in **damnable heresies**, even denying the Lord that bought them, and bring upon themselves swift destruction.

2 And many shall follow their **pernicious** ways; by reason of whom the way of truth shall be evil spoken of.

3 And **through covetousness** shall they with **feigned words** make merchandise of you: whose judgment now of a long time lingereth not, and their damnation slumbereth not.

4 For if God spared not the angels that sinned, but cast them down to hell, and delivered them into chains of darkness, to be reserved unto judgment;

5 And spared not the old world, but saved Noah the eighth person, a preacher of righteousness, bringing in the flood upon the world of the ungodly;

6 And turning the cities of Sodom and Gomorrha into ashes condemned them with an overthrow, making them an ensample unto those that after should live ungodly;

7 And delivered just Lot, vexed with the filthy conversation of the wicked:

8(For that righteous man dwelling among them, in seeing and hearing, vexed his righteous soul from day to day with their unlawful deeds;)

9 The Lord knoweth how to deliver the godly out of temptations, and to reserve the unjust unto the day of judgment to be punished:

10 **But chiefly them that walk after the flesh in the lust of uncleanness**, and **despise government. Presumptuous** are they, **selfwilled**, they are **not afraid** to speak evil of dignities.

11 Whereas angels, which are greater in power and might, bring not railing accusation against them before the Lord.

12 But these, as natural brute beasts, made to be taken and destroyed, speak evil of the things that they understand not; **and shall utterly perish in their own corruption;**

13 And shall receive the reward of unrighteousness, as they that count it **pleasure to riot** in the day time. **Spots** they are and **blemishes, sporting themselves with their own deceivings while they feast with you;**

14 Having **eyes full of adultery**, and that **cannot cease from sin;** **beguiling unstable souls**: an heart they have exercised with **covetous practices; cursed children:**

15 Which have forsaken the right way, and are gone astray, **following the way of Balaam** the son of Bosor, **who loved the wages of unrighteousness;**

16 But was rebuked for his iniquity: the dumb ass speaking with man's voice forbad the madness of the prophet.

17 These are wells without water, clouds that are carried with a tempest; to whom the mist of darkness is reserved for ever.

18 For when they **speak great swelling words of vanity**, they **allure through the lusts of the flesh**, through **much wantonness**, those that were clean escaped from them who live in error.

19 While they promise them liberty, they themselves are the servants of corruption: for of whom a man is overcome, of the same is he brought in bondage.

20 **For if after they** [*those who are taught*]**have escaped the pollutions** of the world **through the knowledge of the Lord and Saviour Jesus Christ**, they are again entangled therein, and overcome, the latter end is worse with them than the beginning.

21 For it had been better for them not to have known the way of righteousness, than, after they have known it, to turn from the holy commandment delivered unto them.

22 But it is happened unto them according to the true proverb, The dog is turned to his own vomit again; and the sow that was washed to her wallowing in the mire.

****

I know this past text is long but I would enjoin the examination of the descriptive phrases. (highlighted or not) Perhaps they shall help in identifying those who should be so labeled.
****

If one thinks back over the last 50 or so years of preaching, and the amount of teaching that has been devoted to false teachers, one unfamiliar with the Bible might envision the subject on every other page! At least! In truth, only **one** specific mention of false teachers is in the Bible. That being the text I used to introduce this part of the study.

JUDE   2Pet. 2, 2Tim 4 without specific reference, and Acts 20:29-30 appear to reference the same type of individual.

It has been my observation over the years that the church has espoused church autonomy. But where "false teachers" are in view, whole congregations may be ostracized or labeled "unfaithful" because of the teachers being used. Brothers! Regardless of our definition of false teachers, **where** is our Bible command or precedent for such action?? The statement has been made; "If you use Bro _____, we won't "fellowship" you"! Or, "I won't be there". (Or use your articles in the "brotherhood paper") Make no mistake, there are things that can and will destroy the

85

local body! But unless those foundational issues are at stake, **what** does our Biblical authority allow or command? One only has authority, and therefore responsibility to act, at **one** congregation. Just because some at one congregation **THINKS** one to be a "false teacher", will not make that true. And if **any** arrogant, Pharisaical spirit is given credence in regard to the "labeling" process, the body of Christ moves one step closer to popery. Or at least becomes one with the "Corinthian" spirit! (I'm of Paul, I'm of Appolos, etc.)

I would pose the question: Of all the teachers in the church today, have **ALL** **ALWAYS** understood, believed and taught as they do today? Were they **all** "wolves in sheep clothing" **then**, but today their "perfect" and advanced knowledge is sufficient to escape that label? What if greater knowledge than we have **now** is attained? Should we not hope and pray for that? Brothers, these questions are not born of derision, but from one who in the past, unwittingly embraced that "perfect knowledge" convoluted reasoning. I (and those who embrace this reasoning) never audibly stated such, but acted as if that were the case. However, not admitting it made me no less guilty!

All erroneous teaching **will** affect the body. **All** fallacious reasoning **will** exact a price. Yet not all erroneous teaching or fallacious reasoning will destroy the body! For example. a congregation may embrace error on the hair subject. They may exclusively use teachers who only teach error on that subject. Yet if one is baptized into that body correctly, believes and practices the truth in that matter, one can be saved. The same is equally true of the "convenience worship" subject! The error taught does not demand the participation of all! Another example. The nature of the indwelling of the Holy Spirit. Exclusive teaching of either position does not demand participation. Why would any one be party to division of brethren, strife or the fracturing of congregations in these matters?! Or any issues such like? Brothers, we need to be more discriminating in the elevating of doctrines the Bible does not elevate. Certainly the "false teacher = false worship" doctrine will **not** stand Biblical scrutiny! See churches of Asia, churches of Galatia, and Corinth. Rebuke, reprove with all longsuffering!!!

Please note in **your** study of false teachers that there are two things in view: <u>personal</u> <u>characteristics</u> **and** the <u>objectives</u> of these individuals. Even though these two things are different, they possess a common denominator.

Biblically, both have in view the aggrandizement and gratification of the false teacher personally!! They feed **ON** the flock! Their intent is to draw away disciples unto themselves! They are dividers! They **cause**, **advocate** or **perpetuate** division of the body! ***FROM THESE, STAND CLEAR!!***

I know some men who I disagree sharply with on several subjects. They teach subjects differently than I do. However, because I know something of the lives of these men, I cannot castigate and demonize them as "false teachers". At the congregation where I have responsibility, I am not afraid of what these men (or others for that matter) **MIGHT** teach. The things I differ with them on will **not** destroy the body. **I** do not know all truth! That's for certain! But I want me, and the congregation to know more than **I** do now! To those men, I would invite: please open the scriptures to us. We will try to search out the things you teach. See Berea

1 Tim 4:1-3
4:1 Now the Spirit speaketh expressly, that in the latter times some shall depart from the faith, <u>giving heed to seducing spirits</u>, and <u>doctrines of devils</u>;

2 <u>Speaking lies in hypocrisy</u>; having their <u>conscience seared with a hot iron</u>;

3 <u>Forbidding to marry</u>, and commanding to ab<u>stain from meats, which God hath created to be received</u> with thanksgiving of them which believe and know the truth.

The following is a list of descriptive terms (from the above text and others) the spirit uses to allow us to understand, define and identify "false teachers".

1. They operate privately and surreptitiously. i.e. by stealth
2. They teach "damnable heresies".
3. They are pernicious. i.e. licentious; no moral restraint
4. They are covetous. i.e. have a greedy desire
5. They use "feigned" words. i.e. fabricated words
6. They use people as merchandise. "trading stock" for personal gain. (or popularity)
7. They desire "tainted" or "impure" things.
8. They disdain authority.

9. They are self-pleasing or arrogant.
10. They are daring.
11. They defy spiritual glory, though knowing its power.
12. They participate in debauchery day and night. i.e. unashamedly
13. They revel in their own delusions. i.e. take great pleasure in the deception they spawn
14. They feel no restraint.
15. They "bait" with a deliberate effort to "trip" the unsuspecting.
16. They exercise their mind to practice extortion and are experts at "overreaching".
17. They follow the way of Balaam. i.e. circumvents God's law and love the wages it pays
18. They use "over-full" words that allure and appeal to the flesh. i.e. flattery
19. They promise freedom from restraint, while making the hearers slaves to corruption.
20. They cause division. i.e. factions
21. They recommend the division of the body.
22. They serve their own belly. i.e. fleshly desires
23. They use mild, pleasant, smooth speech.
24. They desire to mislead the innocent and the young.
25. They "creep in" under cover.
26. They deny Jesus is lord.
27. They can come from within or without.
28. They are grievous wolves. i.e. feeding ON the flock
29. They will "distort" the scriptures. i.e. twist, misrepresent, and corrupt
30. They "distort" the scriptures **in order to** "draw away" learners. i.e. disciples

I suppose one needs to know if one is "guilty" by one descriptive clause, or must all be present to earn the title of false teacher? Brothers, I believe it impossible to make any judgment, or expect any thing close to consensus on who is a false teacher beyond the local body level. Even at that level, there will be errors made. We must not overrun other congregation's liberty or autonomy in making these designations. We must **not** respect (by acquiescence or otherwise) wrong decisions of other congregations. But we must respect their God given right to remain independent in their decision making process! Remember! They stand or fall to their head only. See Rev 2 & 3.

*** A Side Note for Leadership***

To those who are in a leadership position or aspire to it, understand the position. You have no one in front of you (to follow explicitly) except the apostles and Jesus, our head. Even though consideration of events and leadership in other congregations may prove wise, you must not be unduly affected by their choices. Least resistance and tradition have always offered easy choices. You must learn that the sphere of your influence does not allow you to "pressure" (you know what I'm talking about) other congregations or preachers/teachers to "bow at the alter" of your "big" issues! Do not allow others (preachers, teachers, editors, etc.) the opportunity to usurp **your** independent leadership role. Brothers and congregations of the body of Christ are separated when **you** yield to the tendency of leadership in some places to "kow-tow" or "fall in line" on the "elevated" topics. Study the Bible and chart your course thereby!

Church Journals

I have "sideswiped" journals a time or two in this writing. I would like to think there is no relationship between church papers and fellowship/true worship, but indirectly there is. None of these journals proclaim themselves "brotherhood guides". Yet because of weak leadership, and/or lazy study habits, that's what they are allowed to become! I shall not stand in judgment of church journals nor the men that run those publications. I have never read a "church" publication in which I found no insight. However, leadership (and all who read) must scrutinize and investigate these writings as the writings of man. They (editors/publishers) only write what **they think** the Bible says. Their writing and thoughts, by reason of their editorial position, has no more weight than the readers of this or any other treatise. Use those writings (like all religious material) as tools to better understanding and paths to better leaders in the Lord's church. Religious journals must not be used as brotherhood trendsetters or surreptitious edicts!

I know those in the editor/publisher position may possibly read this writing as an affront or attack on them or the publication they run or write for. That is not true. This is simply my effort to convince others of what I believe to be true. Much the same as editors who publish material on a regular basis. I expect this writing to be dissected and parsed the same as the writings in those publications. All of our thoughts and writing **MUST** be subjected to the "assaying" process! Therefore resist the urge to be defensive. I know as well that they feel as "fair game" to every "disgruntled", "sore headed", "disillusioned", "crackpot" the church has known. I am sympathetic but not surprised. It's the "heat" of the "kitchen". Bear it patiently.

Heretick

Titus 3:10-11
10 A man that is an heretick after the first and second admonition reject;

11 Knowing that he that is such is subverted, and sinneth, being condemned of himself.

After much reading, study, and thought, my understanding of heretick, as used in the above passage, will undoubtedly fall short of the reader's desired enlightenment.

However some comment is in order. Even though there is no inherent evil in the term heresy, that is not the case with heretick. One may refer to any choice, or choosing, as heresy without regard to right or wrong. But by the definition, and in context with Titus 3: 8-11, the heretick is an individual who has **chosen** to denounce or turn from that which he **KNOWS (self condemned)** is right! That choice appears to be tantamount to cutting off the "bootstraps" of salvation!

The term, heretick, is most often discussed in relation to false teachers or the word, heresy. But this writer misses the necessity of that relationship. Heretick and "false teacher" do not seem interchangeable or at all synonymous. A heretick may certainly be a false teacher, but a false teacher may not be a heretick.

Anyone identified as a heretick would be found guilty (as always) by the local body to which they are responsible. The Bible will not authorize an "edict" on the brotherhood level. And that includes **ANY** charge that may be brought against a brother or sister. Each congregation must be allowed to "know" the members of that body who are answerable to God **ONLY** for their decisions. The Bible would even authorize warnings about individuals. But those warnings have no power outside the local body. If others do not agree with, nor abide by the judgments of another congregation who has issued that warning, there can be **no (none, zero, zilch, etc.)** legitimate repercussions! Each congregation **MUST** be allowed to make its own independent decisions without fear of censure. Even if they are wrong!!

****

A Related Note

Because of the inviolate nature of autonomy, conflicting decisions on the use of persons or disciplinary actions brought against individuals (teachers and preachers included) cannot be the source of walls and isolationism practiced toward other congregations of the body of Christ! One congregation may **not** agree with the decision of another congregation, but if all the things that make a congregation the body of Christ remain intact, **they shall stand or fall before Jesus**!! There is **not one** instance in scripture that sanctions or authorizes the isolating or alienation of a congregation of the body of Christ!!!

****

Church "Pests" and Seditious Fellows
Acts 24:5

For we have found this man a pestilent fellow, and a mover of sedition among all the Jews throughout the world, and a ringleader of the sect of the Nazarenes:

Gal 5:19-20

19 Now the works of the flesh are manifest, which are these; Adultery, fornication, uncleanness, lasciviousness,

20 Idolatry, witchcraft, hatred, variance, emulations, wrath, strife, seditions, heresies,

Rom 16:17-18

Now I beseech you, brethren, mark them which cause <u>divisions</u> and offences contrary to the doctrine which ye have learned; and avoid them

18 For they that are such <u>serve not our Lord Jesus Christ</u>, but their own belly; and by good words and fair speeches deceive the hearts of the simple

Since the above underlined "labels" were attached to the apostle Paul by his adversaries, the same usage of these terms, or similar ones, today does not insure the correctness of application if intended to "blacken" brothers or congregations. Paul was a pestilence (a plague) to the Jews. And that was good! Paul was accused as a "mover" (a stirrer) "of sedition" (a secular uprising) and that was a false accusation! He was a "ringleader", (leader of the charge) and that was good! And of the sect (a choice) of the Nazarenes, and that was a good choice! He caused division among the true adversary (Acts 23: 6-7) and not among brethren.

Today, if one is in the front line of rebellion against man-made tradition, doctrinal creeds, status quo interpretations, brotherhood hierarchy, or editorial "dictations", one may be looked at just like the Pharisees viewed apostle Paul. As a threat. But that is not necessarily the case. Each congregation or individual needs to have empirical (first hand) knowledge before passing judgment on a brother or sister!!

That having been said, this bit of study is not justification of "pests" nor "seditious" fellows. Truly, "church pests" are a trial and detriment to a congregation. They do disturb the peace and tranquility of the body. And when correctly identified, must be dealt with locally to avoid longer term problems. They, as is always the case, can only be handled at the local body level.

However......

Seditions and heresies in Gal 5, cannot be considered as inane or inoffensive, given their inclusion in the list of the works of the flesh. While we may find ourselves at odds with modern government like Paul, the sedition of Gal 5 is not company to the sedition Paul was accused of.

Sedition in Gal 5 is defined by Mr Strong as coming from compound origin.

Sedition- Def. Strong's 1370 = disunion (*others simply say "division")

From #1364 = twice or two

& # 4714 = a standing

Strong's # 1370 is only used twice in scripture. This text (Gal 5) and Rom. 16:17 where it was aptly translated "division". Therefore when brethren who are true worshippers are divided, the perpetrators and participants are guilty of a work of the flesh. I find it ironic indeed that for years we have tried to correct one work of the flesh, adultery, with the commission of another, seditions!! May God grant us pardon for our errors and humility and wisdom in correcting our mistakes.

HERESY & Pharisees
Acts 24:14

14 But this I confess unto thee, that after <u>the way which they call heresy</u>, so worship I the God of my fathers, believing all things which are written in the law and in the prophets:

Simply labeling a teaching heresy will not make it so! Paul was worshipping and serving in spirit and in truth, but **THAT** way was labeled heresy! He happened to disagree with the religious hierarchy of his day. That was his only problem. The religion of Jesus was referred to as heresy. (def – a choice) But **it** was **correct heresy**! By definition! One who offers heresy is not necessarily a heretick! *A caveat to those who subjugate inspired words to support personal dogma and traditional interpretations!*

Acts 15:5

But there rose up certain of the <u>sect of the Pharisees</u> which believed, saying, That it was needful to circumcise them, and to command them to keep the law of Moses

Acts 26:5

Which knew me from the beginning, if they would testify, that after the most <u>straitest sect of our religion I lived a Pharisee</u>

The Pharisees were leading players in the events and teachings of Jesus. They were aptly named. For Pharisee means "separatist". And separate they were. While we have been called by the gospel and made separate (from the world) unto Christ, we are not at liberty to separate from brothers and sisters who are true worshippers of God. Yet the Pharisaical spirit is still alive and well **IN** the church! It is exemplified at times in the "family" churches that spring up. Most of these do not exist of necessity. Many are within a "stone's throw" of a congregation of believers where true worship can take place. They are just considered too worldly, too weak, too lost, or too "something" to try to worship with or help in some way. It's just much easier to "walk by on the other side".

It is possibly a human weakness to elevate our personal sanctity and holiness by "enlarging our phylacteries" and making sure we pass by "on the other side of the road". If our own perceived holiness is in arrears, it's much easier to "level" those around us than to hold ourselves to a higher personal standard. It's easier to look down our "long skinny noses" at our weak brother and sisters than to endeavor to convince them of error in the spirit of meekness and love. It's easier to point from our "ivory towers" at "those worldly, weak" congregations than to explain in loving and convincing fashion that "it is not lawful to have thy brothers wife"! **(and other much-needed truths)** It is easier to divide congregations than to maintain personal convictions and integrity in the face of opposition. It is easier to "run" from problems and controversy, than to rebuke or reprove. **Even though that is the specific command!** We are **exhorted** to flee from sin, but never from a congregation of the body of Christ!!

It is not possible to rid us of opposition. We need to **learn** how to preserve the unity of the Spirit in the bond of peace! The Pharisaical and divisive spirit among us needs to be quelled. It is the epitome of carnality!

Acts 28:22

But we desire to hear of thee what thou thinkest: for as concerning this sect, we know that every where it is spoken against.

We in the church have long fought against sectarianism. We are forced to regard our exclusive "sect" as non-sectarian even though we will not absolutely deny that other "sects" within the church (commonly referred to as the church of Christ) are <u>not</u> **THE** body of Christ! There were sects among the Jews; but all were Jews. This in **NOT** an attempt to make sects desirable, but rather to change our attitude toward brothers who have not, or hold not the same truths I may be privileged to understand and hold. It is entirely possible to recognize sects among us without becoming sectarian in spirit. **(i.e. everything's alright)** Sects in the body are eliminated by exhortation and reproof! **NOT DIVISION!**

Contending for the Faith

Jude 3-4
3 Beloved, when I gave all diligence to write unto you of the common salvation, it was needful for me to write unto you, and exhort you that ye should earnestly contend for <u>the faith</u> which was once delivered unto the saints.

4 For there are <u>certain men crept in unawares</u>, who were before of old ordained to this condemnation, <u>ungodly men, turning the grace of our God into lasciviousness, and denying the only Lord God, and our Lord Jesus Christ.</u>

Another scripture used to justify nearly every partisan stance and pugnacious spirit that has ever existed. When brothers or congregations parted ways, most has been justified in the name of "contending for the faith". Even in the face of scripture that clearly makes division of true worshippers a sin!

Eph 4:4 states, "there is one faith". Just like one body. (church) Are we to interpret the one "thing believed" of Jude 3 to encompass all things **I**, or a sect with whom I identify, to encompass or epitomize **ALL** the truth?! Allowing me to ostracize, cut off, ignore, disdain, or "disfellowship" any one who strongly (or not so) disagrees?? Brethren, we have seemed to feel "contending for the faith" of verse 3 gives us license for all or some of those things. At the same time ignoring verse 4 that supplies at least **some** restraint by the descriptive phrases used. It has been my observation that the "contending for the faith" that's been done has roughly stopped at that person's, or party's subjective idea of doctrine they believed to be pivotal to their own "brand" of orthodoxy.

False Bretheren and "Cutting Off"

Gal 2:3-4

3 But neither Titus, who was with me, being a Greek, was compelled to be circumcised:

4 And that because of <u>false brethren unawares brought in</u>, <u>who came in privily</u> to <u>spy out our liberty</u> which we have in Christ Jesus, <u>that they might bring us into bondage</u>

Gal 5:11-12

11 And I, brethren, if I yet preach circumcision, why do I yet suffer persecution? then is the offence of the cross ceased.

12 I would they were even cut off which trouble you.

If there was one problem that troubled the churches of Galatia, it would be the men who ostensibly were brethren and surreptitiously were introduced to the church. Today we have stooped to this verse to cut off or banish any brother (or even a sister I suppose) who dared broach a religious "sacred cow" subject. Or disagrees with a partisan doctrine. These people can be "cut off" on just the word of a "trusted brother". It's no wonder we appear pugnacious at times to our denominational neighbors. Brothers can be known as close friends and associates one day, and relegated to "outer Mongolia" the next! All justified on the faulty premise that this text authorizes one person, or sect to "cut off" a brother or whole congregations of the body of Christ because of a single disagreement! And that not even close to a "superstructure" issue.

Brethren, one must admit that the context of Galatians concerns those brethren being wooed by "another gospel". This was a problem that attacked the common salvation and superstructure of the church. We must admit that the things that have caused us the most trouble (and division) over the last 50 years cannot be construed to be of that magnitude. I make that statement knowing full well the importance of godly homes in a congregation. The absence of respect for the marital vow can destroy a home (a person) and weaken a congregation, but the institution of marriage (older than the church) is not to be equated with the church. The **division** that has hobbled the Lord's church for these many years looms bigger than the differences that have spawned that division. Divisions (seditions) are a work of the flesh as is adultery!

2 Tim 4:2-4

2 Preach the word; be instant in season, out of season; reprove, rebuke, exhort with all longsuffering and doctrine.

3 For the time will come when they will not endure sound doctrine; <u>but after their own lusts shall they heap to themselves teachers, having itching ears;</u>

4 And they shall turn away their ears from the truth, and shall be turned unto fables

May God grant us boldness and determination in following vs 2 and to steadfastly resist the temptation to "scratch" our "itching ears"!

Heresies, Contentions, Debate, Strife, and Dispute(s) (ing) Divisions- Heresies- Divisions

1 Cor 11:18-19

18 For first of all, when ye come together in the church, I hear that there be <u>divisions</u> among you; and I partly believe it.

19 For there <u>must</u> be also <u>heresies</u> among you, <u>that they which are approved may be made manifest among you.</u>

As you may have noticed, all of the terms in this major heading are words that bring to mind problems in the body. I believe it to be of paramount importance to correctly understand these terms. Even though unity (with God and one another) is the presupposed desire and goal of all children of God, it is obvious that uniformity of belief on every point of scripture will not be attained in our human state. The question is, how shall we "press toward the mark", while dealing with our immaturity and lack of understanding in spiritual things? Shall division of brethren be a good thing? Must we wink at and overlook sin and error in the body in name of peace?

This treatise is not establishing but rather presupposing the reader's belief in one body. Eph. 4:4 & Col 1:18   I believe these scriptures to be a part of the evidential "framework" of the singular nature of the church! In 1 Cor. 1:13 Paul asks a rhetorical question. Is Christ divided? Obviously (implicitly) answered with a resounding NO! Even though there were differing opinions and a party spirit present at Corinth, how many bodies existed there? That Corinth was divided is absolutely true.

Paul confirms it. But notice again the text at the top of this heading. Paul said there were divisions **AMONG** them! He said there were heresies **AMONG** them! There **were** differences, but the body remained one! Evidently, the differences were not on subjects that define what makes a congregation the body of Christ.

Heresies is a word that religiously has a "black" connotation. Yet when searching the scriptures on this dreaded word, its usage belies its common reputation. The word definition is rather innocuous. Meaning simply, a choice, or to choose. It is only when this word is used in the works of the flesh and coupled with "damnable" in 1 Pet. (discussed in next segment) that we are able to understand that a choice, or to choose, is not always a good thing.

I would refer the reader once again to the opening text of this section of study. 1 Cor. 11:18-19. In light of the whole of Paul's writing to Corinth, one may not construe his statement in vs 19 as a sanctioning of division or heresy. On the other hand we must let Paul's words say all they say. His words were not an advocating of heresy, but rather the inevitable nature of reality ! No escaping it! **Why must** there be heresy **IN** the body? Vs 19 **"For"** (assigning reason) "there must be heresy among you so that (in order for) those who are approved (acceptable-after assaying process) may be made manifest. (or become apparent)

Unless I miss the intent of the words, Paul must have understood that uninspired men must subject their ideas and opinions to the "assaying" process. The truth of the "god-breathed" (inspired) words of scripture will stand the "assaying" process over and over again!! Assaying does not hide truth! But makes "gold" shine like the noon-day sun!!

In Acts 24:14, Paul says that the gospel of Christ was **reckoned** to be "the way called heresy". Alongside of Judaism, the gospel was a choice. A deviation from the status quo. In this case , "the way **called** heresy" was the way of truth! For those who have "assayed" the gospel, there is no longer an intellectual choice. The truth of the gospel has been made apparent!

Therefore heresies and division **may** occur **IN** the body. It is not sought, nor nurtured, but is unavoidable. But woe to those who recommend, perpetrate, perpetuate or condone the division of the body! Even when heresies **are** present!

****

98

Damnable Heresies

2 Peter 2:1-2

1 But there were false prophets also among the people, even as there shall be false teachers among you, who privily shall bring in <u>damnable heresies</u>, even denying the Lord that bought them, and bring upon themselves swift destruction.

2 And many shall follow their pernicious ways; by reason of whom the way of truth shall be evil spoken of.

This scripture has been mentioned under heresy, but it is noteworthy to mention the adjective that makes the "choice" or "choosing" damning or destructible to the "way of truth". Even though this scripture like others has been wrested from its contextual mooring, proper hermeneutics will not let "the way of truth" include **EVERY** Biblical truth! If so, **all** heresy would be damnable heresies. Context rules! Specifically, the "damnable heresy" was "denying the Lord that bought them"!! Correct interpretive rules will preclude heresy from absolute negative connotation when separated from "damnable" or "choices" that do not explicitly threaten the "superstructure" or foundation of the Lord's church.

Sect(s)

Acts 5:17

17 Then the high priest rose up, and all they that were with him, (which is of the <u>sect</u> the Sadducees,) and were filled with indignation,

Acts 15:4-6

4 And when they were come to Jerusalem, they were received of the church, and of the apostles and elders, and they declared all things that God had done with them.

5 But there rose up certain of the <u>sect</u> of the Pharisees which believed, saying, That it was needful to circumcise them, and to command them to keep the law of Moses.

6 And the apostles and elders came together for to consider of this matter

Acts 24:5-6

5 For we have found this man a pestilent fellow, and a <u>mover of sedition</u> among all the Jews throughout the world, and a ringleader of the <u>sect</u> of the Nazarenes:

6 Who also hath gone about to profane the temple: whom we took, and would have judged according to our law.

Acts 26:4-5

4 My manner of life from my youth, which was at the first among mine own nation at Jerusalem, know all the Jews;

5 Which knew me from the beginning, if they would testify, that after the <u>most straitest sect</u> of our religion I lived a Pharisee.

Acts 28:22

22 But we desire to hear of thee what thou thinkest: for as concerning this <u>sect</u>, we know that every where it is spoken against.

Division(s)

John 10:19-21

19 There was a <u>division</u> therefore again among the Jews for these sayings.

20 And many of them said, He hath a devil, and is mad; why hear ye him?

21 Others said, These are not the words of him that hath a devil. Can a devil open the eyes of the blind

John 9:16

16 Therefore said some of the Pharisees, This man is not of God, because he keepeth not the sabbath day. Others said, How can a man that is a sinner do such miracles? And there was a <u>division</u> among them

Cor 1:10-14

10 Now I beseech you, brethren, by the name of our Lord Jesus Christ, that ye all speak the same thing, and <u>that there be no divisions among you</u>; but that ye be perfectly joined together in the <u>same mind</u> and in the <u>same judgment</u>.

11 For it hath been declared unto me of you, my brethren, by them which are of the house of Chloe, that there are <u>contentions</u> among you.

12 Now this I say, that every one of you saith, I am of Paul; and I of Apollos; and I of Cephas; and I of Christ.

13 <u>Is Christ divided?</u> was Paul crucified for you? or were ye baptized in the name of Paul?

1 Cor 3:1-3

3:1 And I, brethren, could not speak unto you as unto spiritual, but as unto carnal, even as unto babes in Christ.

2 I have fed you with milk, and not with meat: for hitherto ye were not able to bear it, neither yet now are ye able.

<u>3 For ye are yet carnal: for whereas there is among you envying, and strife, and divisions, are ye not carnal, and walk as men?</u>

As odious as division is to God and man, the abovementioned scriptures must be allowed to supply insight and understanding on the subject.

Definition: division----Strong"s 4978 _____ split or gap

From 4977_____ to split or sever

Jn 10:19-21describes a division "<u>among</u> the Jews". Yet all remained Jews.

Jn 9:16 describes a division among the Pharisees. But all involved were Pharisees. Who were also a "sect" of the Jews. But all (the divided Pharisees and Sadducees) remained Jews.

1 Cor 1:10 is a clarion call for unity of mind and judgment. This scripture shall preclude the preservation of the status quo so long as that unity is unattained. A congregation whose "unity" is anchored in smug satisfaction, ears "itching" to hear only what they already know to be "the truth", may need to look at Laodicea. Paul (nor this writer) is not advocating division! But understanding its inevitability, gives us insight in dealing with it.

1 Cor 3:1-3 confirms the genesis of division as carnality! And by rhetorical questions, nails down a conclusion! Carnal minds may collide, (or be divided) but the body shall remain one!!

So once again I conclude, define the characteristics of the body of Christ, (previously discussed) and remain united with those who are so defined! Uniformity of understanding in **all** matters has **never** Biblically defined **all** the saved of the ages! But the body he will save. He will save **all** Israel! (not Israel according to the flesh) Rom 9:6 & Rom 11:26.

Debate(s), Disputes(ing), Strife

Rom 1:28-29

28 And even as they did not like to retain God in their knowledge, God gave them over to a reprobate mind, to do those things which are not convenient;

29 Being filled with all unrighteousness, fornication, wickedness, covetousness, maliciousness; full of envy, murder, debate, deceit, malignity; whisperers

Mark 9:33-34

33 And he came to Capernaum: and being in the house he asked them, What was it that ye disputed among yourselves by the way?

34 But they held their peace: for by the way they had disputed among themselves, who should be the greatest

Acts 17:16-17

16 Now while Paul waited for them at Athens, his spirit was stirred in him, when he saw the city wholly given to idolatry.

17 Therefore disputed he in the synagogue with the Jews, and with the devout persons, and in the market daily with them that met with him

Acts 19:8-10

8 And he went into the synagogue, and spake boldly for the space of three months, disputing and persuading the things concerning the kingdom of God.

9 But when divers were hardened, and believed not, but spake evil of that way before the multitude, he departed from them, and separated the disciples, disputing daily in the school of one Tyrannus.

10 And this continued by the space of two years; so that all they which dwelt in Asia heard the word of the Lord Jesus, both Jews and Greeks

Some may feel that this written discussion (worship/fellowship) has strayed from its central thrust. That may very well be the case journalistically speaking. However this writer has seen too many discussions derailed by the wrongful use of these words. Most of the time used out of scripture context and wielded with the finesse of a bull in a china closet. A discussion is usually a discussion until **my** position becomes tenuous or untenable. Then **YOU** are arguing, debating, or wrangling. End of discussion! And for some, end of fellowship!!

What scriptural rule shall award to one sect in the church carte blanc to state with impunity a position held? Then close off deeper discussion under the guise that further "discussion" would be "debating", "strife", "disputing", or "wrangling"? Or that further discussion would be "promoting" or "giving a forum" to false doctrine. It has been the experience of this writer that those whose argument is weak and tenuous are the first to stifle discussion. Let that not be the case for those who profess to seek and promote truth.

Let's investigate these words.

Debate --------Definition = quarreling (by implication wrangling) Strong's # **2054**

Wrangling ----Definition = to argue persistently and angrily; bad tempered argument

Strife----------Definition = a quarrel (by implication wrangling) Strong's # **2054**

Definition = properly, intrigue (by implication, faction) Strong's # **2052**

Intrigue--------Definition = deceitful strategies, a plot

Reprove-------Definition = to confute or admonish   Strong's **#1651**

Confute -------Definition = to persuade or overwhelm in evidential argument

Disputing-------Definition = to investigate jointly   **Strong's 4802** (Acts 6:9)

Definition = mutual questioning   **Strong's 4803** (Acts 15:17)

Definition = to say thoroughly   **Strong's 1256** (Acts 24:12)

Brothers, consider carefully the implication of THE words just defined. Not only shall we be able to tell the difference in wrangling and disputing, but these words shall **EQUALLY** bridle our tongues and constrain our emotions! They must be universally applied to all. These words, by arbitrary use, shall not make void the evidential and authoritative argument of **ANY** sect or person within the body of Christ! Surely, these words properly used (coupled with laws of love) assist us in our pursuit of the "common" salvation. There is room for Godly arguments and disputes. The Bible will allow brothers and sisters the latitude necessary to preserve the unity and **WHOLENESS** of the body as we endeavor to uncover truth !

When shall the elders (older and younger) of the Lord's church lay aside the Corinthian carnality long enough to show to a **LOST** world the **foremost** Bible mentioned characteristic whereby we may be **UNIVERSALLY** identified?!!

THAT YE LOVE ONE ANOTHER!

Just a query in passing.

Do you, dear brother, <u>know</u> to which factions in the body of Christ the abovementioned maxim applies? And which ones are excluded? If not, you/we need to know!

I believe a cursory examination of **debate** and **strife** will allow one to see two things about those words. One. They point to attitude. When self-righteous, haughty, angry, dissentious spirits prevail, a dispute or discussion becomes a debate or strife or both! These are condemned by scripture as fleshly and must not be engaged in.

On the subject of fellowship/worship **and** nearly all other disputes in the church, the manifested spirit of carnality has managed to frustrate the spirit of Christ. Open discussion on many subjects are closed off or avoided under the banner of "it'll cause a split"! Or "we shouldn't argue". Or "it'll cause trouble". Brethren, those who advocate or perpetrate the "division" mentality should not be able to hijack or derail legitimate disputing, arguing or reproof! We need to learn better **HOW** to disagree with our brethren. This is not to support a claim that disagreement is good, but rather an appeal to our spiritual man to treat one another with love and respect, even in disagreements. Disagreements are inevitable but need not be fatal or final! In most church disputing, **mutual** investigating is **not** sought nor desired. But one party (usually the most influential or the majority) declares "the truth" and everything else is declared "strife, arguing and wrangling". End of discussion!!!

It is not reasonable, logical, nor Biblical that the conclusions reached on every subject (convenience worship, adornment, order of worship etc.) should have the same end. Division! The superstructure of the Lord's church does not rest on every issue! Nor does the holding of erroneous doctrine. Nor does the practice of some preclude that congregation from the reception of rebuke or reproof. The fact that consensus cannot not be attained in the present, should not cause all Christians or congregations with whom we disagree to be disenfranchised. (i.e. walled off, isolated. labeled, etc.) Even if a congregation overrules scriptural commands (not involving our identity) God may see fit to send them a "Moses", or a "Phillip", or a "Jonah". He is not willing that **ANY** should perish! "Come, let us reason **TOGETHER**"!

Commonly [mis]used Words in the discussion of Biblical FELLOWSHIP (And other important subjects)

Condone, Fraternize, Compromise, Liberalism, Conservative

In discussing the Bible, words are sometimes used that are **not** contained in the Holy Writ. This segment is not designed as a wholesale condemnation of those words. But rather an examination to make sure that their meaning and usage may be properly supported by scripture. These are freely used in attempts to "color" open discussions on fellowship and true worship. (and many other subjects) They are used to cast aspersions on those who may disagree with "me" or the hierarchy of the day.

For instance. the word, trinity is not used in the Bible. However, in an examination of the term, there appears to be authority to support its use describing or defining the Godhead. Not all terms so used may be as well supported or just be misused.

Let's examine these words.

Condone
Defined: to regard and treat (something blameworthy) as acceptable,
      forgivable, or harmless
  Synonyms: excuse, ignore, let pass, okay, overlook, wink at

In regard to this study (fellowship/worship), condone is most commonly used to describe that which a person is doing when he or she sits among a group of people to worship. And that congregation (or some in it) holds a perceived "false doctrine". Or, if someone in that assembly is known to be a practitioner of error, your presence at that worship service is said to cause **you** to "**condone**" (treat as acceptable or harmless) that sin or error. Anything one knows to exist in that worship assembly, by your presence, causes you to "condone" (hold as harmless or treat as acceptable) that sin! That's the statement or implication made. **Or** is it just **certain** sins (those elevated to "church-splitting" status) one is said to "condone" by sitting in an assembly? We need that list! The same being stated on occasion, when one assembles at a congregation who uses a so-called false teacher. Brothers, we need to get this straight! Uniform understanding and application must be sought. And we must use only the Bible in defining that process!!

One sitting in a worship service with sinners does **not necessarily** equate to fellowship. (participation in others sins) Nor can one's presence in the same assembly with sinners be construed as necessarily condoning (holding harmless) what they do. Nor may one's assembling for worship at a congregation who uses a "false teacher" be equated with condoning **all** that the "false teacher" may embrace. **See Sardis and the churches of Galatia!!** If that were Biblically true on one subject, it would of necessity be true on **ALL** subjects! With very little depth of thought, one may arrive at the effect this would have at ones home congregation. (Where unity on all subjects is not a reality! And may never be!)

Association and proximity is not tantamount to fellowship! Neither can it be construed as the condoning of all things represented in the lives of those present. The Lord ate with sinners. (winebibbers, etc.) And that without having fellowship nor holding as harmless the sins of those he associated with! Those irritated most by the actions of the Lord were the

Pharisees. Whose "separatist" (that's what Pharisee means) and "holier than thou" attitude fell under the stinging rebuke and condemnation of Jesus as much, or more than any other group of people mentioned in the Bible! Beware!!

Jesus came to seek and save the lost! When Christians socialize with the world for pure socialization, Jesus' eating with sinners and winebibbers may not be used as justification for "hobnobbing"! Our problem is our rushing to assign motive to all the actions of our brothers. **All** of "**MY**" associations are for honorable purposes, but all of my brethren are "hobnobbing" with, "condoning", and "fraternizing" if they associate with those I would not!! Right? In spite of its abuse, I think "Judge not that ye be not judged" would arrest the headlong rush to pontificate and malign by our assigning of motive to all who do not have my/your conscience in this matter!

Therefore, for one to condone a sin, one **must** fulfill, in deed, the definition of the word!!

Fraternize
Definition: 1. to associate with others in a brotherly or congenial fashion
2. to associate on friendly term with an enemy or apposing group, often in violation of discipline or orders

A Derivative of Fraternal
Definition: relative to brothers
showing comradeship
constituting a fraternity
biology of

Fraternity
Definition: group organized and associating for a common purpose or interest
state of being brothers
persons of the same class, profession or character

One can see how this word might come in view as fellowship is being discussed and associations are forbidden. But **how** should it be used?

This word is used on occasion to condemn association, or the patronization of assemblies that are considered "off limits". At least by those who feel authorized to arbitrarily set those "limits". I say arbitrarily because there has NEVER been a Biblical rule cited which will allow **all** Christians to walk by the same rule in regards **to** those limits and exclusions. And still respect the autonomous nature of the local body of Christ. Deciding where one **can** (lawful) worship must be concluded by scripture. Those scriptures must be understood and **equally** applied. Deciding where one **will** worship shall remain an expediency!

So what should be thought when stern warnings are issued to those deemed "fraternizing" with "the divorce group", or the "convenience worship" group? Or **any other** "group"?

One of the things that has created and perpetuated a war-like atmosphere in the church is the misuse of words like "fraternizing" being applied to people who do not march in lock step with the "creed", status quo or hierarchy?. In our world, fraternization (aiding or comforting) with the enemies of this nation is considered treason. A high crime punishable by death! When one uses this word, that connotation is clearly present. One must be able with clarity to delineate who is fraternal. (a brother or family) The wrongful usage of the word will allow us to "snub", wall off or condemn (or worse) those with whom we **are** fraternal by definition.

What shall be the fate of those who advise, recommend or insinuate that brothers in Christ are enemies? Or at least "step-children". For this reasoning to resonate, one must conclude that certain congregations are **NOT** the body of Christ or "full fellowship" (Is there a half fellowship?) is not existant, therefore the members of that body are **not** brethren and **cannot**, **must not**, be associated with in **any** way!! To justify what has gone on for 50+ years, one must deny the fraternity of some saints, or admit to an unspoken, (but real) unlawful, congregational "disciplinary" ("let them alone") practice that has made the body of Christ appear sectarian in structure!

Brothers! I know this is redundant, but I must reiterate! By scripture, identify the body! Once we have established the identifying characteristics of the body of Christ, woe [whoa!] to the person who makes enemies of those so identified!!

* By this shall all men know ye are my disciples; if ye have love one for another! Jn 13:35

But the question shall arise: May we fraternize with **all** brothers? 1Cor. 5 has been discussed in some depth. For one to go beyond and illegitimately extend or offer our association to those forbidden in that text (1Cor 5) would violate the intended law of harmony that governs the whole Bible text!

Brotherhood has also been discussed in this writing. In this writer's opinion, that is the nearest Biblical term closely corresponding to the one under consideration in this component of my study. The only direct command concerning this word is: Love the brotherhood! (**AND THERE IS ONLY ONE!!!!!**) To love it one must clearly identify **it**. Do that! And love **it !**

Compromise

Definition: settlement of differences by mutual concession
             agreement reached by adjustment of conflicting or
             apposing claims by reciprocal modification of demands
Synonyms: accommodation, arrangement, bargain, concession, middle
             ground, understanding

In this writer's opinion, as far as character is concerned, there's not much worse than an individual who will compromise truth or one's integrity for the moment, or for personal gratification. (even if I've unwittingly been guilty) Compromise in things inconsequential is a virtue. But in things other than that, a character flaw!

The problem comes to the forefront in the defining of things "inconsequential".

The crux of the matter in regard to fellowship/worship is whether one in some way "compromises truth" when worshiping in an assemblage of brothers and sisters in which resides disagreement or error on some subject. Or perhaps a congregation that has used a preacher inadvisably. It is a foregone conclusion that worshipping with those who do not uniformly believe or practice, (because of growth or intelligence) the same things on **many** subjects **does <u>not</u>** "compromise" truth. We have all done that for years and with ample scripture to prove that true. I know of no one who would contend otherwise.

Where then is the scripture that puts **some** subjects in that category? If some subjects are different, we need that definitive list so that all brothers may be equally bound or free! If your "list" differs with this writer, please share the fruit of your study. It is the belief of this writer that unity with all brothers will **demand** compromise of things inconsequential and longsuffering in all others. The Biblical handling of these matters must reside exclusively in the autonomous authority of the local body. They **must not** be made brotherhood or preacher issues!!

In things sinful that demand my participation, (having fellowship) I will **not** compromise! Nor will I have fellowship (participate) in them!! Christians may **not** accommodate sin! They may **not** make an arrangement **to** sin, or **with** sin!! "Make no provisions for the flesh" They may **not** strike a bargain with sin!!! (or with sinners to accommodate their sin!) The doctrine of Balaam! They may **not** find "middle ground" in things sinful!!!! There is no such rightful territory! They may **not** rightfully come to an "understanding" outside what God-breathed words will support!!!!!

Therefore one sitting in a Biblically defined worship service with a sinner or one who disagrees with another, **shall not,** of necessity, make one a compromiser!

Liberal – Liberalism - Conservative

There probably has not been a subject elevated by discussion or division where the terms liberal (applied to an individual or a congregation) and liberalism (applied to the result of a conclusion reached or a stand taken) have not been liberally applied. Usually by both parties in the discussion. Some of our clichés sound kind of catchy when we use them, but not scholarly when one tries to apply and define them. Some terms are used so frequently and indiscriminately, they cease to have meaning within the context of their definition. This could quite possibly be the case with liberal or liberalism and conservative.

In general, the common usage of this term or label is applied to any one who allows more than **I** will allow. Or participates in things **I** will not. Or in religion, one who knows a lot less than I **think** I know! Religiously, liberal is a term or label often used to polarize, taint and paint Christians one is not personally acquainted with. Brothers and sisters, take time to check out those who seemed continually "painted" (tainted) with the broad brush of labels.

On the other hand, conservative is much more desirable. A "conservative Christian" is reckoned by some to be dull, drab, unexciting and generally cranky and unyielding. But heaven bound nevertheless.

But what **do** the words mean, and are we using them correctly on the brothers and sisters who are the recipients of these labels? **Or,** are we painting with a broad brush dipped in vitriolic paint of our own making? To be applied liberally to those who disagree with "me". Or the subjects I want to be important.

Liberal-Liberalism

Definition: advocates freedom of individual from restraints or restrictions

intellectually independent of tradition or status quo

progressive

not strict; loose

Conservative

Definition: a mindset to preserve existing conditions and institutions or restore traditional ones

limit change

marked by moderation or caution

As much as we (myself included) use these terms, I find it a little strange that the Spirit in His infinite wisdom never saw fit to paint at all with these verbal brushes. And yet as we examine these terms and the definitions that will apply, only vacuous reasoning would allow one to choose one of these labels above the other without regard to subject or context.

By definition, a liberal is free from restraints and restrictions. If the context is circumcision, meats, holydays, etc., Biblically, I **want** to be a liberal. But if the context is fornication, drunkenness, reveling, proper hair,(men and women) etc., I **don't** want to be considered a liberal!

By definition, a liberal is intellectually independent of tradition and status quo. If the traditions we follow are the traditions of Paul, Peter and Jesus, etc. I **don't** want to be a liberal. But if the traditions are of the Pharisees, factions, **ANY** man, I **want** to be a liberal!

By definition, a liberal is progressive. If progressive involves going beyond (or not teaching all) the inspired words, I **don't** want to be a liberal. (Acts 20) If progressive involves "pressing **toward** the mark" or searching for truth unknown to me, I **want** to be a liberal! If progressive leads out of the quagmire of division and confusion, I **want** to be a liberal!

By definition, a liberal is not strict, but loose. The words of the Bible shall one day be our judge. If making those words say **more** than they say, (running ahead, i.e. extremism) is considered "strict", I **want** to be a liberal. If strict or not loose is allowing them to say **ALL** they say and no more, I **don't** want to be a liberal!

By definition, a conservative will strive to preserve existing conditions. (status quo) If the existing conditions are outside the scriptures, I **don't** want to be a conservative. If upon intelligent examination, existing conditions are traditional but outside the scriptures, I **don't** want to be a conservative! If the things I am practicing is wrong, I cannot practice in moderation that which the Bible condemns. I **don't** want to be a conservative. If I am practicing in moderation that which is right, I am conservative!

This part of the study is not designed to make liberal and conservative, words of no consequence, but to allow us to see the futility and counter-productiveness in the wrong use of these terms. Too many times they are used as building blocks for walls of polarization, non-communication, non-association, and isolationism between brethren and congregations of the body of Christ! Don't sow discord among brethren with labels that only serve that purpose! Objectively, we will have to admit that the terms under consideration shall not apply exclusively to any one person or group. Using these terms definitively will require the generalization of the large groups. A patently poor (and probably sinful) way to classify Christians! Or one should use specificity in the subjects (issues) on which you want the "label" to apply.

Furthermore, we should be careful not to usurp the authority of Jesus and "remove" a whole congregation because we see the majority as "liberal/worldly". Search your heart when these labels are applied. If you paint with too broad a brush you may inadvertently "black" the few saints at Sardis. Do not sift out those Jesus shall surely save! Fulfill your responsibility to all congregations of the body of Christ. Preach the word! In season! Out of season! **With all longsuffering !! By the way, that's not tolerance.**

"Extending the right hand of fellowship"

Gal 2:2 6-7 8-9

2 And I went up by revelation, and <u>communicated unto them that gospel which I preach among the Gentiles</u>, but privately to them which were of reputation, lest by any means I should run, or had run, in vain.

6 But of these who seemed to be somewhat, (whatsoever they were, it maketh no matter to me: God accepteth no man's person:) for they who seemed to be somewhat in conference added nothing to me:

In conference (by communing) Paul and the rest found they were preaching the same gospel! Even though there had been no collaboration! Just divine revelation!

7 But contrariwise, when they saw that the gospel of the uncircumcision was committed unto me, as the gospel of the circumcision was unto Peter

Both understanding they were working in the same vineyard, just "plowing different fields"!

8 (For he that wrought effectually in Peter to the apostleship of the circumcision, the same was mighty in me toward the Gentiles:)

9 And when James, Cephas, and John, who seemed to be pillars, <u>perceived</u> the grace that was given unto me, <u>they gave</u> to me and Barnabas <u>the right hands</u> of fellowship; that we should go unto the heathen, and they unto the circumcision.

113

Once again we need to appeal to the context to understand the subject at the center of this conference of chief men. <u>Were both working for the same master?</u> **YES!!** Therefore, we are correct in concluding that "vertical" (God and man) fellowship existed **before** these men met. When they understood (perceived) **that** fact, they also understood their relationship to one another. Fellow laborers **in Christ!**

By the words of the spirit, it is grammatically incorrect to claim an "extension of fellowship". Grammatically they extended the right hands. "Of fellowship" is a prepositional phrase that supplies additional information about the action taking place. In this instance, "of fellowship" allows us to understand the genesis of the action; fellowship! ALL were enjoying the fellowship of God!! Therefore, it is grammatically incorrect to conclude that fellowship "was extended". All authority makes it apparent these men shook hands "in recognition of" fellowship that previously existed. Christian fellowship (horizontal--partners with one another in "the life eternal" in Christ 1Jn 1:7) is not "extended"! It is that which we have based on mutual faith and obedience to the same gospel facts that created fellowship between the men in Gal. 2:2-9. (It was not a handshake!) Preaching the same gospel, serving the same master, believing in the same benefits! True yokefellows and fellow laborers in Christ!

To say that bishops (leadership) have no right to question one not acquainted with in the gospel, would be incorrect. That is their right and responsibility! "Know them that labor among you". But the right of examination should not overreach the scriptural **establishment** of fellowship! (that has already been discussed) They may find out if fellowship exists and acknowledge that partnership, but it is not given to them to extend or withdraw fellowship. The establishment of fellowship must be of scriptural origin and the same for all mankind for all time!

Printed in the United States
78821LV00005B/499-546

9 781434 304056